A COLLECTOR'S GUIDE TO

TV
MEMORABILIA

ANTHONY SLIDE

Also by Anthony Slide
Early American Cinema (1970)
The Griffith Actresses (1973)
The Idols of Silence (1976)
The Big V: A History of the Vitagraph Company (1976)
Early Women Directors (1977; revised 1984)
Aspects of American Film History prior to 1920 (1978)
Films on Film History (1979)
The Kindergarten of the Movies: A History of the Fine Arts Company (1980)
The Vaudevillians (1981)
Great Radio Pesonalities in Historic Photographs (1982)
A Collector's Guide to Movie Memorabilia (1983)
Fifty Classic British Films: 1932-1982 (1985)

With Edward Wagenknecht
The Films of D.W. Griffith (1975)
Fifty Great American Silent Films: 1912-1920 (1980)

Editor
Selected Film Criticism: 1896-1911 (1982)
Selected Film Criticism: 1912-1920 (1982)
Selected Film Criticism: 1921-1930 (1982)
Selected Film Criticism: 1931-1940 (1982)
Selected Film Criticism: 1941-1950 (1982)
Selected Film Criticism: Foreign Films 1930-1950 (1984)
Selected Film Criticism: 1951-1960 (1985)
International Film, Radio and Television Journals (1985)
Selected Theatre Criticism: 1900-1919 (1985)
Selected Theatre Criticism: 1920-1930 (1985)
Selected Theatre Criticism: 1931-1950 (1985)

Pamphlets
Lillian Gish (1969)
Sir Michael Balcon (1969)
The Films of Will Rogers (1979)

Cover Photograph of the RCA TRW-12 Mirror-Lid receiver from 1939 courtesy RCA/International

Cover and book design: Ann Eastburn

Library of Congress Catalog Card Number 84-052272

ISBN 0-87069-440-5
Copyright ©1985
Wallace-Homestead Book Company
10 9 8 7 6 5 4 3 2 1

Published by

Wallace-Homestead Book Company
580 Waters Edge
Lombard, Illinois 60148

One of the
ABC PUBLISHING ⓐⓑⓒ
Companies

Contents

Acknowledgments

Rudy Behlmer, Eddie Brandt, the Companions of Dr. Who, Robert Cushman, Pat De Fazio, Daniel Einstein of the ATAS-UCLA Archives, Robert Gitt, Tom Hatten, Mike Hawks, Margaret Heron of Lawrence Welk Syndication, Cathy Johnson of the Microfilm Library at *TV Guide,* the Library of Congress, the Los Angeles Public Library system, Phil Luboviski of Larry Edmunds Bookshop, Rob McManeus, the Museum of Broadcasting, Frida Schubert, RCA Photo Librarian, Ed Reitan, Fay C. Schreibman of the National Jewish Archive of Broadcasting, Susan Umpleby, the Doheny Memorial Library of the University of Southern California, and Betty White.

Organizations and companies mentioned in the text without an address can be found in the list of addresses at the back of the book.

Introduction

"A television-radio system is like a nervous system," writes Erik Barnouw in *The Image Empire*. "It sorts and distributes information, igniting memories. It can speed or slow the pulse of society. The impulses it transmits can stir the juices of emotion, and can trigger action." Similarly television can, and does, stir our emotions, particularly our nostalgic urges. It recalls events so personal and yet so public as John F. Kennedy's assassination. Through it, we learned of the horrors of the Vietnam War. We shared our lives with television. And television, in a highly individualistic fashion, shared its joys and tragedies with us.

We all loved Lucy, and we wept with joy when she told Desi she was pregnant. Ozzie and Harriet had the perfect, if stuffy, middle-class family, which every American household secretly wished to emulate. We agreed with Robert Young that father did indeed know best. If we sought zany humor, there was always Ernie Kovacs or George Burns and Gracie Allen or Milton Berle. For the children, there was Captain Kangaroo or Howdy Doody. And both children and adults could escape into a fantasy world through "Superman" or into a world of adventure with "Sergeant Preston of the Yukon" and "The Lone Ranger."

If there were problems, they could be left to the Beaver. As one pop singer lamented of this particular folk hero, he died in living color and lived in black-and-white. Black-and-white television was somehow the only real television we knew. How it has all changed. As Sid Caesar commented in *TV Guide*, "Everything nowadays is car crashes. It's all cops and smashing up cars. There are no more comedians in Hollywood; there's nobody laughing any more. Only machines are laughing. The writers don't say, 'Do you think this is funny?' They say, 'How big a laugh do you think this ought to get?'"

Just as the television audience feels nostalgia for the medium's golden age, so has there been an increase in interest in television memorabilia from the 1950s and 1960s. The market for memorabilia is a selective one. It is motivated by personal tastes and, as yet, it has not been over-exploited by the collector-investor acquiring material for deposit in a bank vault to be relinquished for profit in twenty years' time (as has happened with the movie memorabilia market). There is still room in the television memorabilia field for the young collector seeking an elusive issue of *The Man from U.N.C.L.E. Magazine*, for the Trekies (who are a collecting group unto themselves), for the television fan who simply wants to own every issue of *TV Guide*, or for the housewife whose affection for "M*A*S*H" is such that she treasures an autographed photograph of Alan Alda.

Commentator/critic Les Brown has written that, "in commercial television the audience delivers itself, in fairly predictable numbers each hour of the day, no matter what is being televised — a gaggle of soap operas or a presidential address. The audience actually precedes the program; it is the most dependable element in television." Equally dependable is the fact that what an audience chooses to recall with affection and treasure as television memorabilia is only a minute part of television programming. It is highly unlikely that "The Dukes of Hazzard" will ever hold much appeal to memorabilia collectors. What was popular in 1983 will be forgotten by both the general public and most collectors in 1985. The obvious example of genuine, everlasting audience appeal is "Star Trek," cancelled by NBC in 1969 because of a declining audience, but still — some fifteen years later — the series that has generated more television memorabilia, more conventions, and more fan hysteria than any other program.

"Star Trek" falls outside of the golden age of television, which lasted from the early 1950s through the mid 1960s, and its interest to memorabilia collectors is, therefore, somewhat surprising. Most serious television memorabilia collectors tend to limit their interest to the golden age. Of course, television had its origins in the 1800s, with the experiments of Alessandro Volta, André Ampere, George Ohm, Michael Faraday, James Maxwell, Paul Nipkow, and C. Francis Jenkins. In Britain, John Logie Baird developed mechanical television in the 1920s, but the present television system owes its origins to the work of American Vladimir Zworykin, who invented the electronic television camera tube and the cathode-ray tube.

In 1930, both NBC and RCA were providing television demonstrations, and in 1936 television in the United Kingdom became a reality when the BBC opened the Alexandra Palace television station in North London. In 1939, NBC televised the opening of the New York World's Fair, but World War II severely hampered television's forward march. The BBC recommenced television transmission in 1945, and a year later network television came to the United States with the formation of the then-small NBC and DuMont networks. The ABC and CBS networks arrived in 1948, and, with NBC, became the three major American television networks after the demise of DuMont in 1956.

Outside of technical books and manuals, memorabilia relating to the "experimental" period in television's history is almost non-existent. A valid argument might well be put forward that the golden age of television *and* television memorabilia began with the creation of *TV Guide* by Walter Annenberg in 1953, for *TV Guide* is certainly the most enduring of all forms of television memorabilia. Because it is published in local editions, it tends to have a more personal appeal than most national magazines or journals.

For those collectors newly entering the field, there is still opportunity for major, reasonably priced "finds," but interest in this area is growing rapidly. As an example, *Searle's Autographs* regularly lists autographed group

NBC's coverage of the opening of the New York World's Fair by President Roosevelt in 1939. "A" indicates the position of Roosevelt; "B" the location of the NBC camera.

The early years of television in Los Angeles with Don Lee Television. A photograph from August 20, 1945, with popular personality Al Jarvis between the two women.

photographs from series such as "Love Sidney," "Barney Miller," and current shows such as "Cheers." These photographs are sold the same day as the catalogs are received by collectors.

Television memorabilia's new-found respectability and growing interest is further exemplified by recent acquisitions by the Smithsonian Institution's Museum of American History in Washington, D.C. On display here (at what has been described as the nation's attic, but is, more properly, the nation's collective memory drawer) is the jacket Henry Winkler wore as the "Fonz" on "Happy Days;" the studio set from "M*A*S*H;" one of Milton Berle's garish costumes from "Texaco Star Theater;" the police badges, jail door, and roster board from "Barney Miller;" and Archie Bunker's favorite armchair from "All in the Family." In November 1984, Fred Rogers of "Neighborhood" fame presented to the Smithsonian his size 38 red cardigan, made by his mother, for which he exchanges his suit jacket at the start of each show. Its importance to American popular culture is indicated by its display next to a re-creation of a 1915 Cleveland schoolroom and a "Sesame Street" sign.

There are few who can claim to be as old as the motion picture, but many who can make a similar claim with regard to television. Most can identify a certain period, even a specific date, in their lives with a particular television program, series, or event. It is this extraordinary control over our lives and our thinking that makes television memorabilia so personal to each of us. The Smithsonian recognizes television memorabilia as a part of American popular culture. Collectors view it no less importantly as a human and meaningful aspect of their personal lives.

An exceedingly rare photograph issued by the Columbia Broadcasting System to officially announce the start of television at 10:15 p.m., Eastern Standard Time, on Tuesday, July 21, 1931. The personalities are, left to right, top to bottom: Ed Wynn, Ted Husing, Edwin K. Cohan (CBS technical director), Helen Gilligan, Milton Watson, Mayor Walker of New York, Natalie Tower, ("first girl ever exclusively engaged by a network for television"), Kate Smith, Ben Alley, Helen Nugent, and Henry Burbig.

1
The Great Stars

TV Guide is as good an artifact as any with which to begin a book on television memorabilia. Its current covers are usually devoted to a group of players in a drama or situation comedy. In its early years, *TV Guide* featured a television star on its cover. Perhaps the change came about because there are few genuine media stars today. The actors and actresses are famous only because of the series in which they appear. Where or what would John Schneider and Tom Wopat be without "The Dukes of Hazzard?" Who remembers the names of the two actors who replaced this pair briefly a couple of seasons ago? Even Jean Stapleton, for all her years on the Broadway stage, is known to the public at large only as Edith Bunker on "All in the Family." And what success has Carroll O'Connor achieved since the demise of "All in the Family" and the over-rated "Archie Bunker's Place"?

The few television personalities who are household words today owe their fame to the series in which they appear. Two honorable exceptions are Joan Collins, who was a star prior to "Dynasty" and remains a star away from the series, and Larry Hagman, who was an unmemorable actor prior to "Dallas," but is now the best-known and best-loved villain on and off television. For its remaining stars, television must now rely on "old-timers," such as Perry Como or Bob Hope, and celebrities from other mediums, such as country and western's Barbara Mandrell.

Through *TV Guide,* we can recapture television's past in the most pleasant and least taxing fashion. Not only do back issues offer us names and programs from the past, *TV Guide* also tells us what each episode was about, the names of the guest stars, who was popular on local talk shows, and so on. A whole era, otherwise lost to us, is brought back to life.

In itself, *TV Guide* is an extraordinary magazine. It enjoys the largest circulation of any American periodical or newspaper, with some twenty million copies sold each week. It is geared toward a popular audience, yet it often provides articles of a political or thought-provoking nature, usually conservative in orientation. Behind *TV Guide*'s success is Walter Annenberg, its publisher. In 1953, Annenberg purchased and merged three small East Coast television magazines: *TV Digest* of Philadelphia, *TV Forecast* of Chicago, and *TV Guide* of New York. The first issue of the new *TV Guide* appeared April 3, 1953, and the format has never changed significantly. Within a framework of general articles is encased a *local* television guide. *TV Guide*'s popularity is such that it retains its massive circulation despite the fact that local newspapers publish the same basic program information.

Despite its immense circulation, few complete runs of *TV Guide* have survived in libraries, where the magazine has probably been regarded as purely ephemeral, of short-term interest. Once the new issue arrived, last week's issue was discarded. Happily, this situation has led to *TV Guide*'s becoming increasingly valuable to collectors.

However, serious researchers should be aware that microfilm editions of *TV Guide* are available directly from the publisher for any of the 107 current local editions — from Alabama (Northern) to Youngstown-Erie — at $40 per year. The complete microfilm edition of *TV Guide* from 1953 to 1983 costs $1,240. Particularly valuable as an adjunct to any collection of *TV Guide* is the *TV Guide Index 1953-1977,* sold with the five-year *1978-1982 Cumulative Supplement* for $80. The 1983 *TV Guide Index Supplement* is also available for $12. Every article, feature, and review from the journal is included in the index, listed by both subject and author with full cross-referencing. The main 1953-1977 volume contains 45,000 entries. For more information, readers should contact Cathy Johnson of the TV Guide Library at (215) 293-8947.

A July 26, 1952, edition of *TV Digest.* $6.

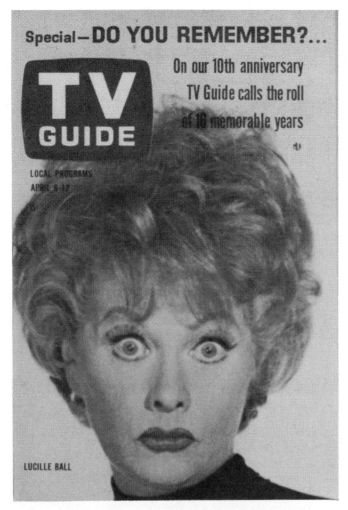

TV *Guide* for the week of April 6 to 12, 1963. $4.

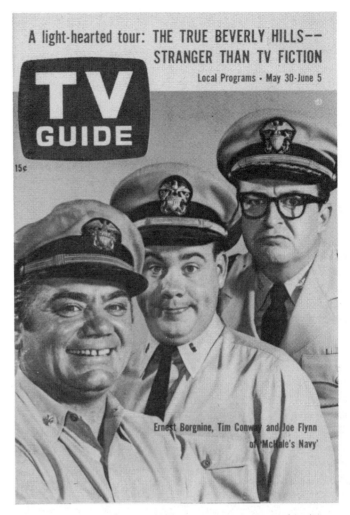

TV *Guide* for the week of May 30 to June 5, 1964. $4.

On the average, issues of *TV Guide* from the 1950s sell for $7 each; from the 1960s for $4; and from the 1970s for $3 or less. However, there are exceptions. Issues with certain stars on the covers can be far more valuable, from $30 and up. Despite the fact that articles and covers are uniform throughout the country, issues for major cities, such as New York or Los Angeles, tend to be more valuable than those from the Midwest or South. Most bookstores specializing in comic books sell *TV Guides*. TV Guide Specialists (Box 20-0, Macomb, Illinois 61455) claims to have every issue available and can locate any article desired. TV Guide Specialists also sells a forty-page illustrated catalog for $4.

Before Walter Annenberg took over *TV Guide*, it was a New York-based fan magazine. Back issues of the original *TV Guide* can sell for as much as $15 each. Pre-1953 *TV Guides* are available from TV Archives (P.O. Box 3, Blue Point, New York 11715).

Copies of the Philadelphia *TV Digest* have been known to sell for low prices. Hampton Books offered a number of them from 1949 at $3 each. However, most local television program guides, usually inserted in the Sunday editions of the newspaper, are hard to locate. Those from the 1950s are worth between $5 and $10 each.

Boston Sunday Post

TV EYE
SEPTEMBER 25, 1955

RICHARD GREENE

Full Week's TV Programs

A typical local television guide, *TV Eye*, September 25, 1955, from the *Boston Sunday Post*. $7.

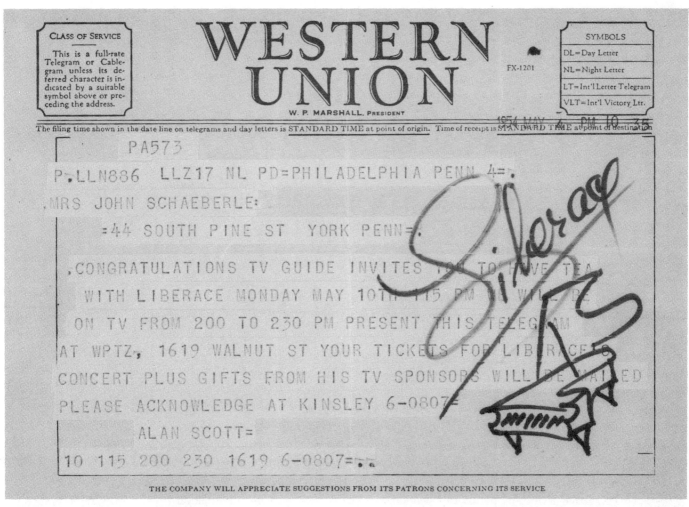

An interesting Liberace autographed item: A 1954 telegram to a winner in the _TV Guide_ "Tea with Liberace" contest in Philadelphia. $12.

There have been a number of anthologies published of articles from _TV Guide._ The best is _TV Guide: The First 25 Years,_ which also offers a good general introduction to the journal by its editorial director Merrill Panitt. For a popular culturist's view of just what _TV Guide_ meant to its readership, Jim Harmon's essay published in _Jim Harmon's Nostalgia Catalogue_ (J.P. Tarcher, 1973) is highly recommended. As Harmon writes, "Color, excitement, romance, information — _TV Guide_ was the best 15¢ worth of magazine since the days of _Spicy Detective_ and _G-8 and His Battle Aces._"

The British equivalent of _TV Guide_ is more staid and older. It is _Radio Times,_ published as a guide to radio and television programming by the BBC since 1923. Current issues are available from BBC Publications (33 Marylebone High Street, London W1M 4AA).

A microfilm edition of every issue of _Radio Times_ from 1923 to 1980 has been published by Chadwyck-Healey (623 Martense Avenue, Teaneck, New Jersey 07666) and is available for $5,425. Microfilm editions of current issues cost $75 per year. Also available from Chadwyck-Healey on microfilm is _The Listener,_ a serious weekly, published by the BBC since 1929; and _Television: The Journal of the Royal Television Society,_ first published in 1928. Other fascinating BBC documents available from Chadwyck-Healey include the newsreaders' typescripts of the Home Service "Nine O'Clock News" 1939-1945; _BBC Radio: Author and Title Catalogues of Transmitted Drama, Poetry and Features 1923-1975;_ and _BBC Televison: Author and Title Catalogues of Transmitted Drama and Features 1936-1975._ Of particular interest is _The BBC Program Index,_ 1979 to present, a comprehensive index to all BBC radio and television programming (available at $180 a year).

Since the 1920s, the BBC has also published handbooks and yearbooks, which are available in this country at extremely low prices. For example, Larry Edmunds Bookshop has copies from the 1920s for as little as $12 each, and from the 1940s for as little as $6 each. Generally, foreign television periodicals sell for very little. It is almost impossible to locate copies of the British Independent Television network's magazine _TV Times_ (247 Tottenham Court Road, London WLP OAU) in the United States, but Hampton Books sold Volume One, August-December 1939, of the German television house organ, _Zeitschrift der Fernseh A.G._ for $75.

Televisions is a little too serious for the enthusiast. Back issues are valued at less than $2.

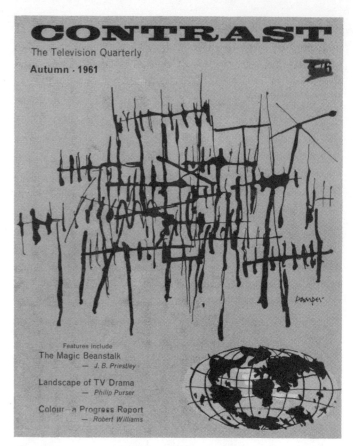

The first issue of the defunct British Film Institute quarterly, *Contrast*, from Autumn 1961. $2.

Other current British television periodicals include:

Broadcast, 32-34 Great Marlborough Street, London W. 1.

Bulletin of the Royal Television Society, Tavistock House East, Tavistock Square, London WCIH 9HR.

Independent Broadcasting, 70 Brompton Road, London SW3 IEY.

Primetime, 275-277 Pentonville Road, London N.W.I.

Television and Home Video, Link House, Dingwall Avenue, Croydon, Surrey CR9 2TA.

TV World, 27 Wilfred Street, London SWIE 6PR.

Despite its name, the British Film Institute is committed to the study and preservation of television. It has published a number of rather pretentious pamphlets on the subject and, from 1961 to 1966, published a serious television quarterly titled *Contrast*. Back issues can still be found in the United States for approximately $2 each. Additionally, the complete run is available on microfilm for a little less than $50 from World Microfilms Publications, 62 Queen's Grove, London NW8 6ER, England.

Current foreign-language television periodicals include:

Altrimedia, MassMedia Edizioni, Via Gaffurio 4, 20124 Milan, Italy.

Millecanali, Via Guido d'Arezzo 19, 20145 Milan, Italy.

Video, Postfach 1042, 7000 Stuttgart 1, West Germany.

Film en TV Maker, Nieuwe Keizersgracht 58, 1018 DT Amsterdam, the Netherlands.

Onda TV, Via Achille Grandhi 46, 2017 RHO Milan, Italy.

Son Magazine, 11 Boulevard Ney, 75018 Paris, France.

Sorrisi e Canzoni TV, Via Angelo Rizzoli 2, 20132 Milan, Italy.

Tele Sette, Via Boschetti 6, Milan, Italy.

Tidskriften TM, Svenska Filminstitutet, Box 27126, 10252 Stockholm, Sweden.

TV Buongiorno, Piazza della Vittoria 15/33, 16121 Genoa, Italy.

Video Actualidad, Infanta Carlota 149, Pral 2a, Barcelona 29, Spain.

Video Aktief, Postbus 16, 6500 AA Nijmegen, the Netherlands.

Video Time, Box 40224, Göteborg, Sweden.

Video Totaal, A.J. Ernstraat 585, 1082 LD Amsterdam, the Netherlands.

Video Uit & Thuis, Postbus 1392, 1000 BJ Amsterdam, the Netherlands.

Videodoc, 24 Rue Bois des Queues, 5976 Incourt, Belgium.

Videokanava, Hepokuja 6C, 01200 Vantaa 20, Finland.

Videopro, 48 Avenue Charles de Gaulle, 92200 Neuilly-sur-Seine, France.

Several Current American television periodicals are:

Broadcasting, 1735 DeSales Street NW, Washington, D.C. 20036. (*Broadcasting* is one of the oldest television journals still published, having first appeared October 15, 1931. In 1982, it published an anthology, *The First 50 Years of Broadcasting*. Back issues seldom appear for sale and can be worth up to $10 each.)

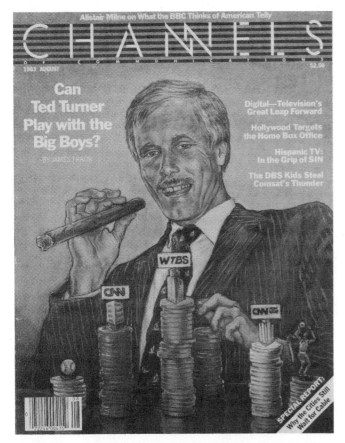

Channels is, with *Emmy*, the best of the current television journals.

Channels, The Media Commentary Council, Inc., 1515 Broadway, New York, New York 10036. (Les Brown's important journal, analyzing television since April/May 1981.)

Nighttime TV, 355 Lexington Avenue, New York, New York 10017.

Television Digest, 1836 Jefferson Place NW, Washington, D.C. 20036.

Television/Radio Age, 1720 Avenue of the Americas, New York, New York 10020.

TV and Entertainment, 1214 S Street SE, Washington, D.C. 20020.

TV and Movie Gossip, 355 Lexington Avenue, New York, New York 10017.

TV and Movie Screen, 355 Lexington Avenue, New York, New York 10017.

TV Dawn to Dusk, Two Park Avenue, New York, New York 10016.

TV Facts, 131 Jericho Turnpike, #401, Jericho, New York 11753.

TV Mirror, 205 East 42 Street, New York, New York 10017.

TV Picture Life, P.O. Box 1133, Dover, New Jersey 07801.

TV Radio Talk, Two Park Avenue, New York, New York 10016.

TV Star Annual, Two Park Avenue, New York, New York 10016.

TV Superstar, 355 Lexington Avenue, New York, New York 10017.

Television Quarterly, with its routinely drab cover, has little interest for the collector. $2.

TV World, 505 Eighth Avenue, New York, New York 10018.

Television Index Information Services publishes a number of useful journals and newsletters edited by Jerry Leichter. They include *TV Pro-Log* and *Network Futures* (both weekly), *Ross Reports Television* (monthly), and *Television Network Movies* (annually). There is no better source for what is in production or planned for television than *TV Pro-Log.* The National Academy of Television Arts and Sciences has published *Television Quarterly,* which is perhaps a little dull and whose articles lack depth, since February 1962. Since the winter of 1979, the Academy of Television Arts and Sciences has published the glossy *Emmy* magazine, a high spot of which is always the "Great Shows" articles. Unfortunately, like *Television Quarterly, Emmy* takes television a little too seriously, refusing to accept that it is "Laverne and Shirley" rather than "Masterpiece Theatre" that television is all about. Walter Annenberg tried to take television a little more seriously than does his *TV Guide* with *Panorama,* but that monthly survived only from February 1980 through May 1981. (A prototype issue was published in July 1979.) Issues of *Panorama* can often be found for sale at $1 or less and should increase in value to at least $3 a copy.

13

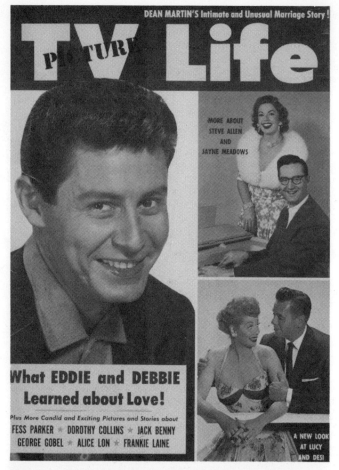

TV Picture Life, February 1957. $10.

TV Song Stars, January 1953. $10.

There is no accurate documentation on just how many fan-oriented television magazines have been published. Some of the earliest are *Radio and Television Mirror* (also known as *Radio-TV Mirror*), published from 1939-1954; *Radio and Television Best* (also known as *TV Screen*), published from 1947-1951; and *Modern Television & Radio* (first published in 1948). Other television fan magazines from the 1950s include *TV & Movie Screen* (first published in 1953), *TV and Screen Life* (first published in 1958), *TV and Screen World* (first published in 1953), *TV Annual* (first published in 1955), *TV Carnival* (first published in 1953), *TV Diaries* (first published in 1956), *TV Illustrated* (first published in 1955), *TV People* (first published in 1953), *TV Personality* (first published in 1954), *TV Pictorial* (first published in 1955), *TV-Radio Annual* (first published in 1953), *TV Song Stars* (first published in 1954), *TV Star Annual* (first published in 1955), *TV Star Parade* (first published in 1951), *TV Stars* (first published in 1951), and *Who's Who in TV & Radio* (first published in 1951).

Other television fan magazines include *TV Album*, *TV Family*, *TV Fan*, *TV Funfare*, *TV Headliner*, *TV-Radio Album*, *TV Times*, *TV World Album* (first published in 1962), *TV: The Television Annual* (first published in 1978/1979), *TV & Movie Album* (first published in 1961), *Radio Stars & Television* (from the 1940s), *Radioland & Television* (from the 1940s), *Inside TV* (first published in 1959), and *Who's Who in Daytime TV* (first published in 1968).

These are exactly the types of periodicals that libraries never bothered to collect. Even the prestigious Library of Congress would discard one issue of a television fan magazine when the next issue arrived. Virtually all television fan magazines from the 1950s are now valued at between $10 and $15 — sometimes a little higher if Elvis Presley or the Beatles are on the cover.

Collectors shouldn't ignore popular magazines, such as *Life*, which would often feature a major television personality as its cover story. Copies of *Life* from the 1950s are well worth $5 each. Also worth checking are obscure semi-serious television journals that came and went in the 1960s and 1970s. At first glance, *TV Author and Reviewer* looks uninteresting, but its April 1960 issue features Rod Serling on the cover and a reprint of the TV script for "Walking Distance" from "The Twilight Zone."

Collectors of television material are now served by a bi-monthly journal titled *The TV Collector* (P.O. Box 188, Needham, Massachusetts 02192), edited by Diane L. Albert. Each issue features an article on a series or personality of the past; an index to episodes of a specific television program; listings of obituaries, marriages, and births; and fascinating classified advertisements placed by collectors seeking videotapes of obscure television episodes. If you want to learn of the Andy Griffith Show Appreciation Society (Box 753, Bermuda Run, North Carolina 27006) or the Barbara Eden International Fan Club (c/o Ken Bealer, 1332 N. Ulster, Allentown, Pennsylvania 18103), *The TV Collector* is the publication for you. A one-year subscription costs $15.

Why Jerry Lewis Is Looking For A Partner

TVBEST

Aug. 25c

 The Page
Patti Tore
From Her Diary

---

*WHY ART CARNEY
HAS TO QUIT
JACKIE GLEASON*

**Things I Never
Told About George**
by Gracie Allen

 **GISELE MACKENZIE:**
**"The Nice
Ones Are
Always
Taken!"**

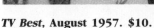

TV Best, August 1957. $10.

TV people

people

TV

people

APR • 25c

ATLAS

DEAN MARTIN
and
JERRY LEWIS

Is JACK WEBB CAUGHT in his own DRAGNET ?

TV People, April 1954. $10.

WHO'S WHO IN
PDC
DAYTIME TV

35ᶜ No. 2

STERLING

THE FIRST MAGAZINE FEATURING ALL THE SERIAL STARS

Joe Gallison

Rosemary Prinz

Mary Stuart

Nancy Hsueh

OVER 1000 PHOTOS & FACTS! • THIS YEAR'S
SCOOP STORIES • Weddings • Babies • Divorces

Eileen Fulton

Ed Bryce

Emily McLaughlin

Carol Roux

GIANT CLIP-OUT DIRECTORY
Real Names • Show Names • Hometowns • Birthdates • Families • Addresses

AT HOME WITH YOUR FAVORITE STARS AND THEIR FAMILIES

Elizabeth Hubbard

Charita Bauer

Jonathan Frid

Ann Flood

Audrey Peters

HOW THE DARK SHADOWS VAMPIRE COMES TO LIFE
THE SHOWS OF THE PAST 25 YEARS

Who's Who in Daytime TV, No. 2 from 1968. $8.

Pinky Lee, a popular television favorite from 1950 to 1957.

Milton Berle, early television's greatest star.

Television's early stars included Lucille Ball, Milton Berle, Faye Emerson, Dave Garroway, Ernie Kovacs, Pinky Lee, Gary Moore, Bishop Sheen, Ed Sullivan, Burr Tillstrom, Fran Allison, and Ed Wynn. The memorabilia they generated ranges from a Soupy Sales button (valued at $10) to a Lucille Ball doll (valued at $100). Milton Berle, beginning with "Texaco Star Theater" on June 8, 1948, is credited with selling more television sets than any other personality. (Eddie Cantor turned that claim into a joke, noting, "It's true. After Berle started appearing on television, my father sold his set, my brother sold his, my sister sold hers.") Milton Berle was the first entertainer to appear simultaneously on the covers of *Time* and *Newsweek* (on May 16, 1949). Those two issues are now collector's items. Berle was best known for his grotesque characterizations and his appearances in female attire, and yet such photographs of the comedian are exceedingly hard to find. They're valued at far more than the $5 maximum price of a regular photograph of Berle.

An autographed photograph of Milton Berle can sell for between $10 and $15. In fact, autographed material of the early television personalities is the easiest and best to collect. Addresses for all living celebrities can be found in the *Ultimate Movie, TV, and Rock Directory,* compiled by Roger and Karen Christensen (and published by the Cardiff-by-the-Sea Publishing Company, P.O. Box 909, Cardiff-by-the-Sea, California 92007). The book must be ordered well in advance of publication; a new edition goes out of print almost as soon as it appears. For up-to-date information on addresses of television and film personalities, a subscription to *Newsreel* is highly recommended, as is membership in the Manuscript Society (c/o Audrey Arellanes, 1206 North Stoneman Avenue, #15, Alhambra, California 91801) and the Universal Autograph Collectors Club (P.O. Box 467, Rockville Centre, New York 11571). Collectors should not overlook such obvious sources for addresses as *Who's Who in America, Contemporary Authors,* and other personality publications. For a current star, a request for an autographed photograph in care of the celebrity's network can sometimes get results, but generally such mail does not reach the celebrity. Under no circumstances should a collector risk sending original photographs or artwork to a television personality in care of a network or local television station.

Faye Emerson COLORING BOOK

A Faye Emerson coloring book, published by Saalfield of Akron, Ohio, in the early 1950s. $8. Faye Emerson had her own show, "Faye Emerson's Wonderful Town" (CBS, 1951-1952), and was also a panelist on many 1950s quiz programs, including "I've Got a Secret," "Masquerade Party," "Quick as a Flash," and "What's in a Word."

Despite his popularity, autographed photographs of Benny Hill are exceedingly difficult to find in the United States. $25.

Jane Wyman as Angela Channing, and Mel Ferrer as Phillip Erikson on a 1982 episode of the CBS series "Falcon Crest."

Good sources for autographed material include Robert F. Batchelder, La Scala Autographs, Jerry S. Redlich, and Sy Sussman. Sy is also able to provide 8×10 photographs of many television personalities for as little as $1 each. Other major suppliers of TV celebrity portraits — both past and current — include Eddie Brandt's Saturday Matinee, Collector's Bookshop, Larry Edmund's Bookshop, Movie Star News, and Stephen S. Sally. The average price for an original photograph of a television personality is $3.50, and collectors should not really expect to spend more than $5. There are exceptions, of course, such as photographs of Benny Hill, which are almost impossible to find in either the United States or the United Kingdom. Addresses for Hill and other British television personalities can be found in *The British Film & Television Year Book* (available at most major libraries).

Early material relating to television personalities does turn up on the market from time to time. In 1980, a collection of television scripts and sheet music belonging to Eddie Fisher sold for a mere $375. An early letter from Jane Wyman can be worth $100 — far more than an autographed photograph of the actress in her current television success, "Falcon Crest." Of course, autographed television material can also decrease in value. How many people remember who shot J.R. on "Dallas"? It was Kristin Shepard, played by Mary Crosby, whose autograph was highly desirable for a while, but is now virtually unsalable. At the same time, who remembers who played Mrs. Shepard on the series in 1979? It was Martha Scott, an actress whose career embraces television, theatre, and the motion picture, and whose autograph will always be desirable.

Elvis Presley is another personality whose television career was secondary to his work in other fields. Yet videotapes of his television appearances continue to sell well, though they're not as popular as videotapes of the Beatles' first appearance on "The Ed Sullivan Show" in 1964. Television fan magazines from the 1950s with Presley on the cover are valued at between $12 and $15. Most extraordinary are the three issues of *TV Guide* from September 8-14, September 22-28, and September 29-October 5, 1956, featuring a three-part article on Presley. Those issues sell for between $35 and $80 each. Other issues of *TV Guide* featuring Presley are similarly overpriced.

To posthumously celebrate Presley's fiftieth birthday, RCA Records issued a six-record set titled "Elvis — A Golden Celebration," which includes all of the entertainer's television appearances from the mid-1950s. RCA Vice-President Gregg Geller explained, "Ever since the shows were telecast, I'd subscribed to the belief shared by most Presley fans: What a crazy company RCA is. This stuff is *great*, why not put it out? The fact is, RCA didn't have the material to put out. The Steve Allen shows were the property of his production company, Ed Sullivan Productions owned those shows, and so on. We had to negotiate with each company individually."

The best information on Elvis Presley memorabilia can be found in *Elvis Collectibles* by Rosalind Cranor, published in 1983 by Collector Books (P.O. Box 3009, Paducah, Kentucky 42001). It sells for $12.95.

The antithesis of Elvis Presley, but a bulwark of American television, is Lawrence Welk, whose programs on ABC and in syndication from 1955 through 1971, provided viewers with a rare opportunity to enjoy the last vestiges of American vaudeville. The Lennon Sisters, Myron Floren, Bobby Burgess, Arthur Duncan, Norma Zimmer and Alice Lon (the last and first Champagne Ladies), Jo Ann Castle, Joe Feeney, Anacani, Tom Netherton — they are all part of the Lawrence Welk family and all intrinsic parts of American television history. In the 1950s, the Welk family was regularly featured in fan magazines. Since 1979, Wolf Products has published a full-color Lawrence Welk calendar. Like all calendars, which are so easily disposed of at the end of the year, these are guaranteed to become collector's items. Attractive color brochures were once available to promote the television series and for distribution to the live audience. *Village Notes,* published out of the Lawrence Welk Village in Escondido, is well worth collecting, as are the products sold by Lawrence Welk Presents (1299 Ocean Avenue, Suite 800, Santa Monica, California 90401). Included in the catalog are Lawrence Welk song books and picture albums, Lawrence Welk playing cards, and Lawrence Welk pewter thimbles, spoons, and dinner bells.

A 1982 edition of The Lawrence Welk Musical Family Calendar, last produced in 1984, and guaranteed to become collector's items.

TV Radio Mirror, April 1958. $10.

The Lennon Sisters, the best-known members of the Lawrence Welk musical family. From left to right: Kathy, Janet, Peggy, and Diane, featured on the show from 1955 to 1968.

Lawrence Welk with his most recent champagne lady, Norma Zimmer, who was first featured on the show in 1960.

Filming "The Lawrence Welk Show" from the now-demolished Aragon Ballroom in Santa Monica, California.

One type of television personality who has a higher opinion of himself than does the average viewer is the newsreader or reporter. Hugh Downs and Dan Rather published autobiographies some years ago. Recently Bill Kurtis and Jessica Savitch wrote their autobiographies — books quite definitely destined for a quick trip to the remainder table. Presently, photographs of major news personalities sell between 50¢ and $2 each. Eventually, those of a Dan Rather or a Walter Cronkite could well be worth as much as $5 each, particularly if the photographs have connections with important news events, such as a presidential primary.

It is easy to overlook the importance of local television personalities and the delight they have given viewers through the years. A good example in Los Angeles is Tom Hatten, who joined KTLA as a staff announcer in the early 1950s and from 1956 to 1964 hosted the station's "Popeye and Friends," which featured Popeye and other cartoons and Hatten in a sweatshirt and sailor's cap. As to memorabilia, Hatten recalls:

"You must remember that those shows were done with practically no budget. All the money that was spent was spent on the cartoons. The hosts all worked for scale, or we were on staff as announcers. It was just another part of our job — we didn't get extra money for it. Television was new to most people and there wasn't an awful lot of competition. So we didn't get into the premium business. The kids got a sailor hat when they came on the show, and we sent out decals, which were provided by King Features, owners of the copyright to the Popeye character."

Hatten remembers a change in 1962, when cartoon shows were lagging in popularity. Rock and roll was stealing much of the audience in the late afternoon time period. Hatten's show went off the air in August 1964. Today Tom Hatten pursues an acting career on stage and screen and is still at KTLA, hosting "Family Fun Festival" on Saturdays and Sundays and a new Popeye series, revived in 1975. Hatten makes sketches of the Popeye characters and sends them out if kids specifically ask for a picture of Popeye and Olive Oyl.

"However," says Hatten, "we don't have any sort of premium that would give us an idea of how many people are watching, the way they used to in the early days with radio shows. The Little Orphan Annie pins that they sent out from Chicago in the 1930s probably cost them 10¢ to make and were worth it to the sponsor, Ovaltine. Now *Time* magazine will send you out a radio if you subscribe for six months. If they can afford to do that, we can afford to do something even on a local basis."

Hatten participated in the golden age of television at the national level, too, having appeared in a "bit" part in the first episode of "I Love Lucy." "I think I got twenty-five dollars," says Hatten. "I and a lady named Ingrid Goude — who was Miss Sweden of, I think, 1952 — were at a table at the Tropicana Club. Ingrid had been at NBC a couple of days before (they shot the show at NBC although it was a CBS program). She had one brown eye and one blue eye, and they used her in early NBC color tests. We sat at a table and

Local Los Angeles television personality Tom Hatten, photographed in 1957 and 1982. The ship's wheel featured in the 1957 photograph is from "Reap the Wild Wind." The photograph was taken in Paramount's portrait gallery by Bud Fraker.

applauded when Desi came out and sang. I wasn't so fond of him, but I thought Lucille Ball was terrific. I loved her in *Du Barry Was a Lady* and particularly in *Best Foot Forward*."

One of the first shows on which Hatten appeared was the Al Jarvis program on Channel 13 in Los Angeles. Jarvis' "girl Friday" was Betty White, who delighted early television audiences with "Life with Elizabeth" (syndicated from 1953-1955) and later as Sue Ann Nivens on "The Mary Tyler Moore Show" from 1973-1977. A few years ago, it was possible to purchase 16mm prints of "Life with Elizabeth" for as little as $25 each. Today they are rare, and even Betty White does not have a complete run of the show. She reiterates Tom Hatten's comments that local television generated little memorabilia. What Popeye memorabilia was created had nothing to do with the television shows, but was licensed by King Features.

Hatten says that "kids are very apt to join a club of some sort now if it has some sort of modern fillip to it." This is certainly true in connection with a Los Angeles program, in which Elvira (actress Cassandra Peterson) introduces horror movies. Seen on KHJ-TV (Channel 9), "Movie Macabre" offers viewers the opportunity to join the Elvira Fan Club. In the first seven weeks 2,500 people signed up, and the membership cards, photographs, and bumper stickers generated by the fan club will eventually increase in value.

Taken as a whole, local television programming has never been particularly worthwhile or honorable. One exception was, and is, KTLA in Los Angeles. It is perhaps appropriate that, in 1985, KTLA was the first local television station to be honored with a retrospective tribute at the Museum of Broadcasting in New York.

The big night for television's stars — be they writers, directors, producers, or actors and actresses — is the Emmy Awards. First presented on January 25, 1949, the Emmy Awards have since grown. Only six statuettes were awarded on that first night, but now there are separate Emmy Awards presentations for daytime television, local programming, and technical achievements.

The Emmy Awards were initially presented by the National Academy of Television Arts and Sciences (NATAS), but in 1976 a dispute developed between the Los Angeles and New York chapters of the Academy. Eventually a new Academy of Television Arts and Sciences (ATAS) was created in Los Angeles. That organization presents the Emmy Awards for nighttime television, while NATAS is responsible for the Emmy Awards for daytime television, sports and news programs, and local programming. NATAS publishes a cumulative *Emmy Awards Directory*, providing complete information on Emmy award winners and nominees from 1948 on in all categories. A similar directory for the nighttime Emmys is published by ATAS for the awards since 1978. Long out of print (and out of date) is Paul Michael's and James Robert Parish's *The Emmy Awards*, published by Crown in 1970, and valued at $15 or more.

Photographs from the Emmy Awards presentations are difficult to locate. Even the two academies do not have photographic files going back to the first awards. Photographs are valued at $5 each or more (depending on the year and the personality in the photograph). I wonder how many people remember the winner of the very first Emmy for Most Outstanding Television Personality of 1948? It was Shirley Dinsdale, who appeared with her puppet Judy

Splinters on KTLA. Because of her obscurity, photographs of Dinsdale are almost impossible to locate and are worth as much as $10 each.

Programs from Emmy Awards presentations can be worth up to $12.50 each. Collectors should also be aware of programs from other television-related shows, such as the Oscar telecast. These programs sell for as much as $10 each, but recent copies can be purchased directly for $5 each from the Academy of Motion Picture Arts and Sciences, 8949 Wilshire Boulevard, Beverly Hills, California 90211. Also collectible are programs for television tributes, such as the Television USA Program at New York's Museum of Modern Art from 1962 (valued at $7.50) and the 1972 "BBC 50th Anniversary Tribute" at London's National Film Theatre (worth $5).

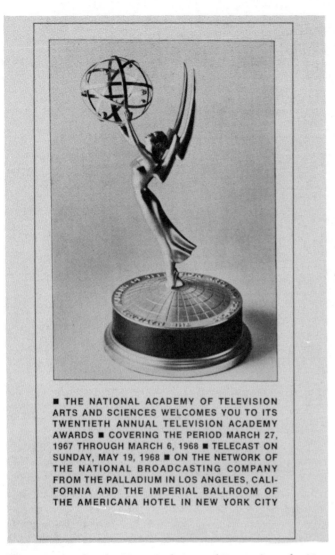

■ THE NATIONAL ACADEMY OF TELEVISION ARTS AND SCIENCES WELCOMES YOU TO ITS TWENTIETH ANNUAL TELEVISION ACADEMY AWARDS ■ COVERING THE PERIOD MARCH 27, 1967 THROUGH MARCH 6, 1968 ■ TELECAST ON SUNDAY, MAY 19, 1968 ■ ON THE NETWORK OF THE NATIONAL BROADCASTING COMPANY FROM THE PALLADIUM IN LOS ANGELES, CALIFORNIA AND THE IMPERIAL BALLROOM OF THE AMERICANA HOTEL IN NEW YORK CITY

The program for the Twentieth Annual Emmy Awards, May 19, 1968. $6.

The Hollywood Foreign Press Association presents awards to television personalities. John Conte (accepting for NBC's "Matinee Theatre"), George Gobel, and Ralph Edwards.

*To Tony —
with great
affection —
Betty White
& Stormy*

Betty White, an endearing television personality, who first became popular with national audiences on "Life with Elizabeth," 1953 to 1955.

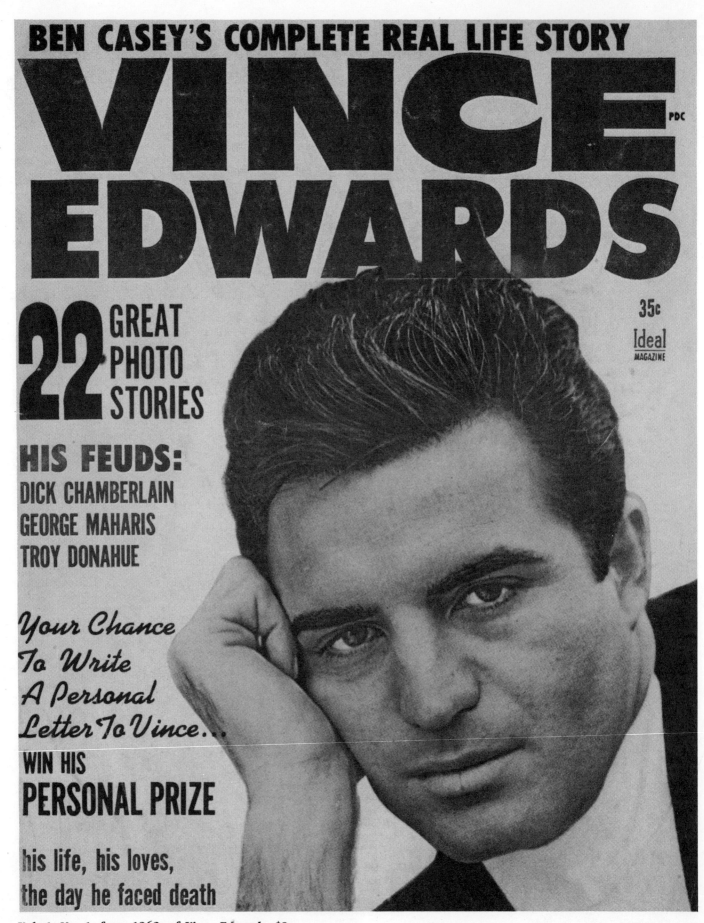

BEN CASEY'S COMPLETE REAL LIFE STORY

VINCE EDWARDS

PDC

22 GREAT PHOTO STORIES

35c

Ideal
MAGAZINE

HIS FEUDS:
DICK CHAMBERLAIN
GEORGE MAHARIS
TROY DONAHUE

Your Chance To Write A Personal Letter To Vince...

WIN HIS PERSONAL PRIZE

his life, his loves,
the day he faced death

Vol. 1, No. 1, from 1962, of *Vince Edwards*. $9.

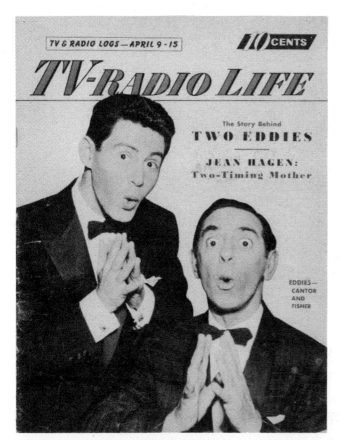

TV-Radio Life, April 8, 1955. $10.

Burr Tillstrom with Kukla and Ollie (where's Fran?) in a photograph from 1961.

Two television pioneers: Ed Wynn and Gary Moore.

Jack Lescoulie and Dave Garroway on the "Today" show in 1960. Florence Henderson is the woman perched by the monitor.

Betty White with Georgia Engel on "The Betty White Show," ABC, 1978.

An unusual historic photograph taken on the set of the Mike Douglas Show; autographed by Steve Allen, John Cameron Swayze, Mike Douglas, Jayne Meadows, Fran Allison, and Burr Tillstrom. $25.

Wink Martindale on "The New Tic Tac Dough," 1978.

Sports commentator Howard Cosell was the host of a 1975-1976 ABC series, "Live . . . from New York City . . . It's Saturday Night Live with Howard Cosell."

Ted Mack, host of "The Original Amateur Hour" from 1948 to 1960.

Television's perennial juvenile, Dick Clark, photographed in 1955.

Johnny Carson welcomes Henry Winkler to "The Tonight Show."

2
The Great Shows

George Reeves on "The Adventures of Superman" (1952-1957).

Robert Shayne, who played Inspector William Henderson on "The Adventures of Superman" is still around to sign photographs such as this one, valued at $5.

The standard reference work for anyone interested in the history of television shows and series is *The Complete Directory to Prime Time Network TV Shows, 1946-Present* by Tim Brooks and Earle Marsh (published in hardcover and paperback by Ballantine Books). It's more than 800 pages list television shows from almost the last forty years.

If asked to determine which shows are all-time cult favorites as far as memorabilia collectors are concerned, I would select the following twenty-four shows — eight from ABC, five from NBC, five from CBS, four syndicated, and two that played on multiple networks.

ABC: "The Addams Family" (1964-1966), "The Adventures of Ozzie and Harriet" (1952-1966), "Batman" (1966-1968), "Bewitched" (1964-1972), "The Bionic Woman" (1976-1978), "The Lone Ranger" (1949-1957), "77 Sunset Strip" (1958-1964), and "The Six Million Dollar Man" (1974-1978).

NBC: "Bonanza" (1959-1973), "Dragnet" (1952-1970), "Lassie" (1965-1967), "The Man from U.N.C.L.E" (1964-1968), and "Star Trek" (1966-1969).

CBS: "The Beverly Hillbillies" (1962-1970), "Dallas" (1978 to present), "I Love Lucy" (1951-1961), "Mr. Ed" (1961-1965), and "Sergeant Preston of the Yukon" (1955-1958).

Syndicated: "The Adventures of Superman" (1951-1957), "The Cisco Kid" (1950-1956), "Kukla, Fran and Ollie" (1948-1976), and "The Muppet Show" (1976-1981).

Multiple Networks: "Leave It to Beaver" (CBS and ABC, 1957-1963) and "Tom Corbett, Space Cadet" (CBS, ABC, and NBC, 1950-1952).

I include "Dallas" not because there is a vast quantity of memorabilia generated by the show throughout the country, but because it has generated an extraordinary volume of "instant" souvenirs in the Dallas area, as anyone who has passed through the Dallas-Fort Worth airport will testify. "Dallas" has also spawned the Dallas Traveling Museum, which has toured twelve cities, displaying such artifacts as the gun that shot J.R. Ewing, Sue Ellen's wedding dress, and Bobby Ewings's belt buckle. As *TV Guide* asked, "Who says America ain't got culture?"

It is worth noting that many of these shows do not come from the so-called golden age of television, and it is equally worth noting that the majority do not represent the best of television. Indeed, it might be argued that many represent American television at its worst! To those readers who find my list of top twenty-four programs depressing, I can only refer them to Richard Hoggart's response to the question, "Can educational television ever hope to command as large an audience as "Gunsmoke?" in *The New York Times* (November 4, 1962): "The answer is, of course, 'No.' They can't, and it would be a queer society in which they could; or in which gardening programs or book programs or ballet programs — no matter how good they were — attracted anything like the audience that a variety show gets. If we approach the problems of broadcasting in that way, we are sure to end in excessive depression."

Television *is* a trashy medium. Nothing can alter that fact. It is the medium of "Dance Fever" and "Knot's Landing." Viewers own a television receiver in order to watch that type of programming, not to enjoy what Public Broadcasting in America laughingly propagandizes as educational or "cultural" shows (which usually means that Alistair Cooke and a highly paid camera crew filmed an introduction to a series which was shown on television in the United Kingdom without benefit of opening and closing comments). Is it simply that the British are more intelligent than Americans and do not need to be told what has happened, is about to happen or will happen, or could it be that PBS has money to waste?

Perhaps not surprisingly, PBS has produced little in the way of television memorabilia. Still photographs from "Brideshead Revisited" are prized, largely because of the fan following for Jeremy Irons. A poster designed by Edward Gorey for "Mystery" sells for $25. Robin Ellis has authored an obscure book on the making of the "Poldark" series. It was published in Cornwall, the English county in which the program is set. "Upstairs, Downstairs" was responsible for a Mrs. Bridges, (the cook played by Angela Baddeley) brand of "old-fashioned" English foods, such as preserves and plum puddings. Until fairly recently, these were available in specialty shops in the United States. The containers may well increase in value.

There is endless variety to the memorabilia relating to specific television programs. It can range from a book such as *Mr. Peepers: A Sort of Novel* by Wally Cox (published in 1955 by Simon and Schuster and valued at $15) to a green felt hat sold in connection with "The Adventures of Robin Hood" (CBS, 1955-1958), an English series featuring Richard Greene in the title role. (The hat is now worth $25). There are games from long-forgotten quiz programs, such as "Yours for a Song" (ABC, 1961-1962). The Bert Parks "Yours for a Song" game from 1962 is worth $20. There are cut-out paper dolls featuring Gale Storm in "My Little Margie" (CBS and NBC, 1951-1955) worth $30 or Edd "Cookie" Byrnes in "77 Sunset Strip" (ABC, 1958-1963) worth $35.

"M*A*S*H" (CBS, 1972-1983) has been the most popular series on American television. Keep in mind, though, that there are far more television sets, and, hence, far more viewers in the 1980s than there were in the 1950s. "M*A*S*H" has been discussed in many books, notably *M*A*S*H: The Exclusive Inside Story of TV's Most Popular Show* by David S. Reiss, which includes profiles of the players and producers, and a history of the show, with a detailed listing of all 193 "hilarious and poignant episodes." More sumptuously produced is Suzy Kalter's *The Complete Book of M*A*S*H*, which is of special interest because it lists "M*A*S*H" Products — everything from pencil cases, hats, and rainwear (in Australia only) to boys' pajamas and dartboard games. "M*A*S*H" is a good example of a recent television series from which the show's owner and producer, Twentieth Century-Fox, has been careful to license anything and everything. It not only licensed American-produced products, but also foreign items merchandised with specific regard to the country. Even the trivia books, published by New American Library, are licensed by Twentieth Century-Fox. As recently as March 1983, Royal Orleans and Twentieth Century-Fox offered a limited edition "M*A*S*H" commemorative plate for sale at $25. Such heavy and copyright-controlled merchandising may well mean that "M*A*S*H" items will not increase substantially in value.

Wally Cox and Tony Randall on "Mr. Peepers" (NBC, 1952-1955). This photograph is from October 1953.

The original stars of the long-running CBS night-time soap opera, "Dallas" (first televised in 1978). From left to right: Patrick Duffy, Victoria Principal, Jim Davis, Barbara Bel Geddes, Charlene Tilton, Larry Hagman, and Linda Gray.

"M*A*S*H," first seen on CBS in 1972, was the most popular series on American television.

The first television series to generate a considerable volume of memorabilia, including T-shirts, dolls, comic books, lunch pails, figurine coloring kits, and even sets of dominoes, was "It's Howdy Doody Time." Between 1947 and 1960, 2,343 Howdy Doody shows were made. Behind Howdy Doody was a former vaudevillian, Buffalo Bob Smith, whose other characters included Dilly Dally, Phineas T. Bluster, Flubadub, and Clarabell. "Parents found it noisy and mindless but expensive, since their children wanted all the products it displayed," wrote *Life* (May 7, 1971). "They couldn't stop it, though; it was defiantly, joyously, for kids only."

Running a close second to "It's Howdy Doody Time" is "I Love Lucy," which generated comic books (valued at $5 each), cut-out paper doll sets of Lucy, Ricky, and Ricky, Jr. (valued at $40 each), and various Baby Ricky items. There are numerous books on "I Love Lucy" (see separate listing) as well as the I Love Lucy Fan Club (1646 Eleventh Avenue, San Francisco, California 94122). An excellent article on "I Love Lucy" collectibles, "On the Air: I Love Lucy" by Richard Friz, appeared in *Collectibles Illustrated* September/October, 1983, pages 82-86.

Rod Serling's "The Twilight Zone" (CBS, 1959-1965) has never lost its popularity with television audiences. According to *The Twilight Zone Companion,* there are some two-and-a-half million copies of the three *Twilight Zone* collections in print, over ten million *Twilight Zone* comics, and *Rod Serling's Twilight Zone Magazine* has been a popular item on newsstands since 1981. "Death Valley Days" (syndicated, 1965-1966) is of interest because the host for those years was Ronald Reagan, who also hosted "General Electric Theatre" (CBS, 1954-1962). "Alfred Hitchcock Presents" (CBS and NBC, 1955-1965) helped create an audience for issues of the *Alfred Hitchcock's Mystery Magazine,* which have become collector's items, valued at $5 and more.

The British Monty Python troupe has been honored with a number of books, the best of which is *Life of Python* by George Perry. Despite the fact that the show is seen in America only on tape, one episode on 16mm film is for sale from Canterbury Films (26 Rivers Drive, Great Neck, New York 11020). The print is not of the best quality, but that particular show does include the "Spam Song." Canterbury also sells a 16mm and Super 8mm Alfred Hitchcock television promo reel, in which the master of suspense introduces his television shows.

One of the first television series to be filmed in color was "The Cisco Kid." An autographed photograph of Duncan Renaldo in the title role sells for $20, while an illustrated booklet issued in connection with Renaldo's personal appearances sells for $5.

"Buffalo Bob" Smith with his best-known creation, Howdy Doody.

Lucy and Ricky with their neighbors, Fred and Ethel Mertz (William Frawley and Vivian Vance) on "I Love Lucy."

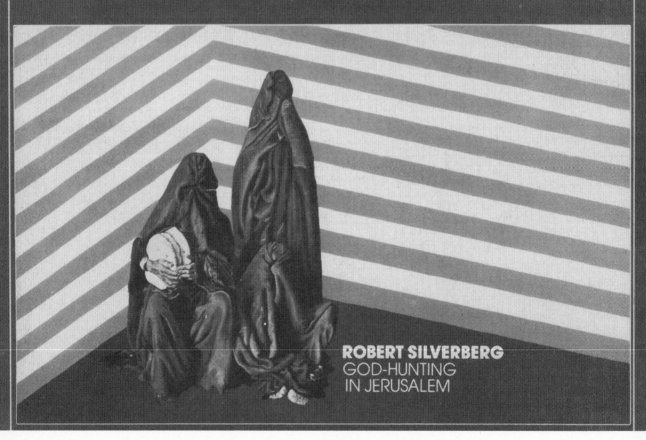

A DOZEN ORIGINAL STORIES

ROD SERLING'S
THE TWILIGHT ZONE MAGAZINE

JULY 1981 / $2

ALL-NEW TALES OF SUSPENSE, HORROR AND THE SUPERNATURAL IN THE TRADITION OF THE TELEVISION SERIES

ROBERT SHECKLEY
DEATH IN THE SWAMP

RON GOULART
ZOMBIES IN THE BAYOU

STANLEY SCHMIDT
HORROR ON THE CAMPUS

CHARLES L. GRANT
TERROR IN THE SNOW

TALES OF
MOON MADNESS
MAGIC SPELLS
FRIENDLY MONSTERS
HAUNTED HOUSES
AND A VISIT
TO DREAMLAND

**ROD SERLING'S
CLASSIC TZ CHILLER**
'EYE OF THE BEHOLDER'

EXCLUSIVE INTERVIEW
**SUPERMAN'S
RICHARD DONNER**
TALKS ABOUT DIRECTING
'THE TWILIGHT ZONE'

TALES OF "SMILEY"
BY STEVE ROSSE

**SHOW-BY-SHOW GUIDE
TO TV'S TWILIGHT ZONE**

ROBERT SILVERBERG
GOD-HUNTING
IN JERUSALEM

Rod Serling's The Twilight Zone magazine, July 1981, Volume I, Number 4. $3.

Another former member of the Monty Python troupe, Michael Palin, also has his own BBC series called, "Ripping Yarns." It was first seen on PBS in 1985. Palin is seen here with Clifford Kershaw in "The Testing of Eric Olthwaite."

An autographed photograph of Bob Denver and Alan Hale, Jr., stars of "Gilligan's Island" (CBS, 1964-1967). $15.

The Cleaver Family (Barbara Billingsley, Hugh Beaumont, Jerry Mathers, and Tony Dow) on "Leave It to Beaver" (1957-1963).

Robert Young as Marcus Welby, M.D., with James Brolin as Dr. Steven Kiley (ABC, 1969-1976).

A famous 1976 episode of "All in the Family," in which Archie Bunker (Carroll O'Connor) discovers the woman whose life he saved is really a man (Lori Shannon).

Curiously, the closer an item is to the show itself, the less it seems to be worth. An autographed photograph of the principals in "Hill Street Blues" can sell for $15, but an original script from the show sells for only $3.50. There is simply no market for television scripts of a recent vintage, and they are easily obtainable for less than $5 from Book City Collectibles or Collectors Book Store, both in Hollywood. Earlier TV scripts are more difficult to locate and subsequently more highly valued. An original script from "Leave It to Beaver" or "I Love Lucy" could sell for $25 and up.

A lucrative area of television memorabilia collecting is that of autographed group photographs from popular series. These photographs often are offered for sale by Searles Autographs and other dealers. An autographed cast photograph from "Barney Miller" can cost $22.50; from "Cheers," $45; and from "Love, Sidney," $10. An autographed photograph of Art Carney and Joyce Randolph in "The Honeymooners" sells for $20, while one of Art Carney and Jackie Gleason sells for $22.50. Vintage photographs of Jerry Mathers in "Leave It to Beaver" have been fetching as much as $30 each. An autographed photograph of Robert Young in "Father Knows Best" is worth $15; the addition of two more cast members to the photograph raises the value to $22.50.

Since his 1978 murder, autographed photographs of Bob Crane in "Hogan's Heroes" have steadily risen in price, until they now sell for as much as $30 each. Autographed photographs of Clayton Moore as the Lone Ranger vary in price between $5 and $12.50. A few years ago, the Wrather Corporation, owners of the copyright for the Lone Ranger character, committed a despicable act by refusing permission for Moore to appear as the masked man. Since Jack Wrather's death, however, the company has rescinded its action. During the period in which Moore was under court restraint, he was forced to pose wearing sunglasses rather than a mask, and I suspect photographs of Moore in that guise will eventually become more valuable than those of Moore fully masked.

Autograph prices seem to bear little relevance to the ages of the personalities involved. An autographed photograph of Carroll O'Connor in "All in the Family" is worth $18.50, as much as an autographed photograph of Tom Selleck in "Magnum, P.I." O'Connor has already achieved permanent cult fame and the value of his autograph will not decrease. But if Selleck loses some of his current sex-oriented appeal, his autographs could become less valuable in years ahead.

Comparisons between the different stars of the same show are interesting, if perhaps odious to the stars involved. Desi Arnaz's autograph is worth only $10, compared to $15 for that of Lucille Ball, even though there are far more Ball autographs in circulation than Desi Arnaz autographs. Autographs from "M*A*S*H" actors illustrate the relative popularity of the various cast members. The signatures on photographs of Jamie Farr, Loretta Swit, and Alan Alda sell for $18.50 each. Harry Morgan's autographed picture is worth only $15.

An autographed photograph of Clayton Moore as the Lone Ranger. The show was seen on ABC from 1949-1957, although John Hart took over the title role from 1952-1954. $7.

ALL YOU'D LIKE TO KNOW ABOUT

ALL IN THE FAMILY

A FAWCETT PUBLICATION
No. 1
75 CENTS

THE
ONLY
AUTHORIZED
MAGAZINE
TO TAKE
YOU
BEHIND
THE
SCENES
WITH
THE
BUNKERS!

FAMILY
ALBUM
PHOTOS

INTIMATE PROFILES
EXCLUSIVE STORIES

By Marcia Borie

Few people are aware that "All in the Family" generated this 1971 Fawcett publication, *All You'd Like To Know About All in the Family.* $5.

40

Aside from autographed photographs, it is usually possible to find signed contracts relating to individual shows. These are interesting, if not particularly glamorous, items. Irene Ryan's contract in connection with "The Beverly Hillbillies" sold recently for $60. A contract covering a 1976 appearance by Orson Welles on "Dinah!" sold for $85. Bear in mind that autographs on contracts must always be authentic, whereas the same is not necessarily true of autographs on photographs — particularly photographs that were "signed" and mailed while a major star was at the height of popularity.

A few years ago, it was possible to find photographs covering the entire history of American television for fifty cents or less. Today, photographs from the early years of television are becoming harder and harder to locate, while photographs from even recent series sell for $3.50 each. Despite dwindling stocks, particularly in the latter's case, the two best sources for television photographs remain Eddie Brandt's Saturday Matinee and Larry Edmunds Bookshop, both located in Los Angeles.

Original memorabilia from television series can sometimes wind up in curious places. Toy versions of Jack Webb's badge, No. 714, as Sergeant Joe Friday on "Dragnet" (NBC, 1952-1970) can still be found for under $20. The original badge, along with scripts and other items relating to both the television and the radio series, were donated by Webb's widow to the Los Angeles Police Department, which plans to display some of the material at its Police Academy. The scripts and tapes of the radio programs (from 1940-1953) can be used by the public, by appointment, through the Public Affairs Section, Office of Special Services of the Los Angeles Police Department (150 North Los Angeles Street, Los Angeles, California 90012).

An autographed photograph of Anthony Geary may currently be worth $15 but, generally, autographed material from soap opera stars will not increase in value. Today's detergents may also be yesterday's detergents, but yesterday's soap opera performers will not be tomorrow's. There are many books on television soap operas (see the Bibliography) and there are also a considerable number of periodicals, all of which indicate the continuing popularity of the genre if not the genre's stars. Soap opera journals are well worth collecting. They include *Afternoon TV* (Two Park Avenue, New York, New York 10016), *Daytimers* (105 Union Avenue, Cresskill, New Jersey 07626), *Daytime Serial Newsletter* (P.O. Box 6, Mountain View, California 94042), *Daytime TV* (P.O. Box 1133, Dover, New Jersey 07801), *Soap Opera Digest* (420 Lexington Avenue, New York, New York 10017), and *Soap Opera Stars* (355 Lexington Avenue, New York, New York 10017).

The one soap opera which became a permanent cult favorite is "Dark Shadows," telecast on ABC from 1966-1971. It spawned two feature films from M-G-M: "House of Dark Shadows" (1970) and "Night of Dark Shadows" (1971). A Gothic mystery series involving families in the nineteenth and twentieth centuries, the show's best-known star was Jonathan Frid, who portrayed Barnabas the vampire and overshadowed the soap opera's intended star, Joan Bennett.

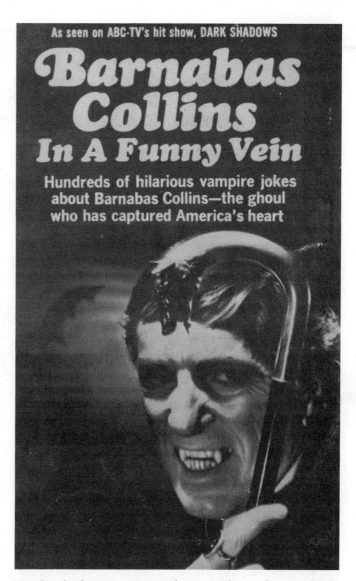

As seen on ABC-TV's hit show, DARK SHADOWS

Barnabas Collins In A Funny Vein

Hundreds of hilarious vampire jokes about Barnabas Collins—the ghoul who has captured America's heart

"Dark Shadows" generated a number of paperback volumes, including this 1969 edition of vampire jokes, published by Paperback Library. $4.

"Dark Shadows" is the only soap opera to have generated a multitude of memorabilia, including records, games, comic books, paperback novels — even bubble gum.

"Dark Shadows" spawned a comic strip and comic books, published by Gold Key. The first issue of the latter, complete with poster, is valued at $7. Milton Bradley produced a Barnabas Collins Dark Shadows Game in 1969, which is now worth $30. Also, there were two series — the first with a red border and the second with a green border — of "Dark Shadows" wallet photos and bubble gum. A complete collection is worth $25.

Paperback Library published a set of thirty-two *Dark Shadows* novels, as well as a book of humor titled *Barnabas Collins in a Funny Vein* (published in 1969 and valued at $4). Also valued at $4 is *The Dark Shadows Cookbook*, compiled by Jody Cameron Malis and published by Ace Star Books in 1970. The L.P. of "The Original Music from ABC-TV's Dark Shadows," played by the Robert Cobert Orchestra and issued on Philips PHS-600-314, can be found for $6. Exceedingly rare are the 45 r.p.m. records relating to "Dark Shadows," particularly the Philips 40648 recording of "I Wanna Dance with You" and "Theme from Dark Shadows," played by the Robert Cobert Orchestra. It sold at auction a couple of years ago for $90.

Walt Disney cartoons had been used for television experiments back in the 1930s, but the Disney organization first came to modern television December 25, 1950, with "One Hour in Wonderland." The Walt Disney series was first seen on ABC on October 27, 1954, and has been a staple of television programming, moving over to NBC in 1961, to the present. Additionally, "The Mickey Mouse Club" dominated ABC children's television from 1955-1958. Both of these series generated considerable memorabilia.

"The Mickey Mouse Club" sponsored *Walt Disney's Mickey Mouse Club Magazine,* a Mickey Mouse Club Annual, record albums, posters, logos, T-shirts, hats, cut-out Annette Funicello dolls, and much more. From the Walt Disney series came Davy Crockett and Zorro, with resultant memorabilia such as the famous Davy Crockett coonskin hat, pocket knives, and lunchboxes, and the Zorro hats, masks, and whip set, manufactured in 1959 by M. Shimmel Sons. As with all Disneyana, anything connected with Disney's television programming can only increase in value. A Mickey Mouse Club musical cookie jar from the 1950s can sell for $85. A box of Mickey Mouse or Davy Crockett straws, also from the 1950s, can sell for $25. All of the Disney television memorabilia is documented in Cecil Munsey's *Disneyana: Walt Disney Collectibles* (Hawthorn Books, 1974).

If any group of characters has supplanted the Disney creations in the hearts and minds of children — and, for that matter, adults — it is the Muppets. These creations of puppeteer Jim Henson became popular on "Sesame Street," but came into their own with the British-produced "The Muppet Show," syndicated from 1976-1981. According to *The Complete Directory to Prime Time Network TV Shows,* Jim Henson made his first network appearance in 1957 on "The Tonight Show," with Kermit the Frog singing "I've Grown Accustomed to Your Face" to Nebel, the purple monster. The Muppets now have their own publication, *Muppet Magazine* (300 Madison Avenue, New York, New York 10017), first published in January 1983, and Muppet toys are available at any toy shop. Today they may be commonplace, but in years to come they could prove to be the nostalgic television memorabilia of the 1990s.

"Star Trek" was seen on NBC from September, 1966 through September, 1969. It was not a particularly popular show — otherwise NBC would not have cancelled it. But it became a cult favorite and came back to life as an animated cartoon series and as a series of feature films. All but the first of those films managed to capture the same simplistic approach to life in space, that has given the original television series continuing appeal in reruns. Somehow "Star Trek" presented a world of the future that seemed worth considering — a world closer to a 1930s vision of the future than to the sterile, futuristic vision of a "Star Wars."

Some episodes of "Star Trek" have been available on videotape for a number of years, as has a blooper reel (which is not particularly entertaining or amusing). In December 1984, Paramount Home Video announced the release of all seventy-nine original, uncut television episodes of "Star Trek," priced at $14.95 per sixty-minute program, along with the release on videotape of the movie "Star Trek III: The Search for Spock." Thus "Star Trek" is the first television series to be available in its entirety on videotape.

There are now some twenty legitimate books dealing with "Star Trek" (see the Bibliography), including *The Official Price Guide to Star Trek and Star Wars Collectibles.* Also available are a number of paperback stories based on the "Star Trek" scripts, including the most famous, "The Trouble with Tribbles," by David Gerrold.

"Star Trek" fans should join Starfleet, the international "Star Trek" club, which has ninety-two chapters scattered throughout most major cities in the United States and publishes *Communique.* Further information can be obtained from Fran Booth at P.O. Box 63008, Westmore, Texas 78163.

Many chapters also publish journals, such as *Archenar Innercon* (32936 Kelly Lane, Yucaipa, California 92399), *Constitution Comments, Genesis,* and *Unlimited Horizons* (all from 49 Stima Avenue, Carteret, New Jersey 07008), *Clarion* (P.O. Box 3742, Ontario, California 91764), *Jupiter Log* (1126 South Willow Lane, Springfield, Missouri 65804), *Attention All Hands. . .* and *Off Duty* (2387 Richmond Road, Cuyahoga Falls, Ohio 44221), *Potempkin Dispatch* and *Potempkin Revelation* (739 Hill Avenue, Pittsburgh, Pennsylvania 15221), *To Boldy Go. . .* (5328 Watkins Road,

STARFLEET
COMMUNIQUÉ
Volume Three — Issue One

graphic art by Eric A. Stilwell

Roddenberry Interview — Page 4
The Motion Picture Re-reviewed — Page 10

Starfleet Communique, **published by Starfleet. This issue features an intelligent interview with "Star Trek's" creator, Gene Roddenberry.**

Millport, New York 14864), and *Starfleet Trinary Information Center* (817 North 9th Street, Petersburg, Illinois 62675). Readers should also be aware of the National Star Trek and Man from U.N.C.L.E. (there's a combination!) Club, at P.O. Box 21413, Reno, Nevada 89515. There is also an International Clearinghouse for Star Trek Information (Box 12, Saranac, Michigan 48881) and Starfleet Command (1012 Northwestern Drive, Grand Forks, North Dakota 58201). For those not as anxious as the U.S.S. Enterprise to journey where no man has gone before, it should be stressed that all addresses are on the planet earth — even if some of the fans might appear to be somewhat off of it.

The major source for "Star Trek" memorabilia is Lincoln Enterprises, which publishes a catalog billed as a "passport to a galaxy of authentic collector's items." The catalog includes Star Trek bumper stickers, T-shirts, stationery, newsletters, coloring books, calendars, decals, and posters

"Space Patrol's" Nina Bara (who played Tonga) is still around to sign photographs. $5.

(including one of Spock and former President Nixon, and one of President Reagan and a Klingon). Lincoln offers scripts for $7.95 each. Also available are Vulcan crystals (mounted in a ring at $4.95) and assorted Command insignia jewelry.

Lincoln Enterprises also sells scripts from creator Gene Roddenberry's "Spectre," "Questor," and "Genesis II." Here also are scripts from "Kung Fu" (ABC, 1972-1975), most at $6.50 each; and from "Search" (NBC, 1972-1973), most at $3 each.

There is, of course, much "Star Trek" memorabilia not available from Lincoln, including a set of "punch out" sheets offered as a promotional premium by Milky Way candy, now worth approximately $20; the Random House "pop-up" books featuring "Star Trek" adventures, valued at $10 each; and a late 1970s wristwatch with Spock on the dial, worth $25. Aside from television memorabilia, considerable memorabilia is generated by the motion pictures, including film stills, posters, lobby cards, books, and novelty items.

"Star Trek" has its origins in "Space Patrol" (ABC, 1951-1952) and "Tom Corbett, Space Cadet" (CBS, ABC, NBC, 1950-1951). Among the memorabilia related to the former are space binoculars and smoke guns, valued in the hundreds of dollars. Wheat Chex and Rice Chex featured "Space Patrol" cards, which now sell for $10 or more. One of the original stars of the series, Nina Bara (who played Tonga), is a regular fixture at many Los Angeles paper shows and is happy to sign autographs and her own story of the "Space Patrol" saga. Mass produced by the Hanover (Pennsylvania) Glove Company in the early 1950s, Tom Corbett Space Cadet gloves are exceedingly rare, as are the same company's Tom Mix gloves. Robert Gitt, now director of preservation at the UCLA Film Archives, recalls persuading his father, Harry N. Gitt II, owner of the company, to produce the gloves because he enjoyed the series so much. Gitt also recalls his chagrin when the show was cancelled and his father lost a good deal of money from having overproduced the gloves. According to Gitt, these were basically cowboy gloves for kids, with Saturn printed in silver dye on black leather and with different colored fringes. Among other Tom Corbett items are "inter-planet, two-way phones," ID bracelets, and wristwatches, valued at $100 each. *The Tom Corbett Wonder Book of Space* from 1953 is worth $25.

The one British program that has generated major cult appeal in the United States was "Doctor Who." It began November 23, 1963, and became the most popular series in the history of British children's television. With his police telephone box turned into a spaceship called the Tardis, the obligatory scarf draped around his neck, and a penchant for a British candy called jelly babies, Doctor Who was responsible for almost as many clubs and amateur fan journals as "Star Trek."

William Shatner as Captain James T. Kirk and DeForest Kelley as Dr. Leonard "Bones" McCoy on "Star Trek."

The cast of ABC's "Space Patrol" (1951-1952).

"Doctor Who" novelty items, including a talking K-9, a talking Dalek, and a "Doctor Who" game.

Among the books available relating to the series are Peter Haining's *Twenty Years of Doctor Who,* Mark Harris' *The Doctor Who Technical Manual,* Terrance Dicks and Malcolm Hulke's *The Making of Doctor Who,* Alan Road's *Doctor Who — The Making of a Television Series,* and John Tulloch and Manuel Alvarado's *Doctor Who: The Unfolding Text.* Marvel Comics publishes *The Doctor Who Monthly,* the British edition of which is infinitely superior to the American. The BBC publishes a *Doctor Who Annual,* but gone are the days when one could walk into the BBC's London headquarters and ask for and receive complimentary photographs of the Doctor. The *Doctor Who* stories were published originally in hardcover editions by W. H. Allen, with the first being *Doctor Who and an Unearthly Child* by Terrance Dicks in 1981. Paperback editions of the stories are published by Target Books (available in the United States from Lyle Stuart, 120 Enterprise Avenue, Secaucus, New Jersey 07094). "Doctor Who" enthusiasts warn against purchasing Americanized editions of the stories, which not only use Americanized spellings and phrases, but, far worse, have the Doctor enjoying jelly beans rather than jelly babies.

To the general public, "Doctor Who" is probably best known for its distinctive theme music, produced by the BBC Radiophonic Workshop and composed by Ron Grainer; and for the Daleks, the science fiction monsters introduced in the first series, featuring William Hartnell as the Doctor, and created by Terry Nation. The theme music was in the British Top Ten a few years ago in a "pop" version by Mankind on Motor Records. BBC Records has produced L.P.s of "Doctor Who: The Music" and "Doctor Who: Sound Effects." In 1979, the BBC released "Genesis of the Daleks," a complete 1979 radio broadcast, written by Terry Nation and featuring Tom Baker as the Doctor. Dalek toys are still available in the United Kingdom, but will undoubtedly become collector's items. A few years ago, it was possible to purchase at "Doctor Who" conventions such British imports as a Doctor Who Game of Time and Chance, a battery-operated Palitoy brand talking Dalek, and a battery-operated Palitoy brand talking K-9. Today the last two are probably valued at $30 each.

Six actors have portrayed Doctor Who. They are William Hartnell, Patrick Troughton, Jon Pertwee, Tom Baker, Peter Davison, and Colin Baker. Hartnell died in 1975, but the rest are alive, and their addresses can be found in the *Ultimate Movie, TV and Rock Directory.* It is curious but perhaps not unexpected that all have achieved greater fame as Doctor Who than as any other character they played in their careers.

The major fan club for Doctor Who enthusiasts is the Companions of Doctor Who (P.O. Box 56764, New Orleans, Louisiana 70156). Founded in September 1981, the Companions has over fifteen hundred members and publishes *Time-Log* and *The Unpaid Scientific Advisor.* The major British source for "Doctor Who" memorabilia is John Fitton of Hensall. Geppi's Comic World (1720 Belmont Avenue, Bay C, Baltimore, Maryland 21207) offers a complete selection of Target Books, as well as the Doctor Who Tardis Bank

Tom Baker as "Doctor Who," with his ubiquitous spaceship, the Tardis.

($5), a Doctor Who Pencil Case ($6.95), a Doctor Who Button Set ($14), and the Doctor Who Game of Time and Space ($17.95).

A complete listing of dealers in "Doctor Who" memorabilia is available from the Companions of Doctor Who, but other sources worth mentioning are Forbidden Planet (23 Denmark Street, London WC2H 8NN, England; and 821 Broadway, New York, New York 10003), Intergalactic Trading Company (P.O. Box 1516, Longwood, Florida 32750), and New Fantasy Shop (5651 West Belmont Avenue, Chicago, Illinois 60634). There are more than twenty amateur fan magazines devoted to "Doctor Who," including *The Fourth Incarnation of Doctor Who* (c/o Ellen Farris, 1503 35th Avenue North, Birmingham, Alabama 35207), *Jelly Baby Chronicles* (39 Bennett Street, Pontiac, Michigan 48058) and *Travelling Companions* (c/o Susan Sizemore, 6421 26th Street West, St. Louis Park, Minnesota 55426). More than thirty fan clubs dedicated to the preservation of "Doctor Who" include American Fans of Jon Pertwee (c/o Linda Terrell, P.O. Box 25, Dunedin, Florida 34296), Doctor Who Fan Club of America (P.O. Box 6024, Cherry Creek Station, Denver, Colorado 80206), First Official Doctor Who Fan Club (c/o Brian Smith, 61 Whitelaw Road, Dunfermline, Scotland KY11 4BN), the Patrick Troughton Preservaton Society (P.O. Box 1764, Petersborough, Ontario K9J 7X6, Canada), and the Tom Baker Friendship Group (c/o Gwynth Bland, 67 Longford Avenue, Feltham, Middlesex TW14 9TH, England).

Despite the ongoing popularity of "Doctor Who" in the United States, the series continues to be seen only spasmodically on public broadcasting and cable stations. No "Doctor Who" videotapes are legitimately available for sale, but, of course, fans tape the shows whenever they are telecast and are more than happy to exchange their tapes with other enthusiasts.

Aside from "Star Trek" and "Doctor Who," there are fan clubs for a number of other television series and for a considerable number of television personalities. A good listing can be found in the *Ultimate Movie, TV, and Rock Directory*. Information can also be obtained from Trina Trinajstick at the National Association of Fan Clubs, 2730 Baltimore Avenue, Pueblo, Colorado 81002.

The world of children's television has generated an extraordinary amount of toy and "throw-away" memorabilia, which continues to increase in value. The best source for such material is Lynn Becker of La Mirada, California. Among the items listed in recent catalogs have been novelties relating to the Lone Ranger and Tonto, Bullwinkle, Rocky, Dudley Do-Right, Herb Shriner, Howdy Doody, Bozo the Clown, Batman and Robin, Starsky and Hutch, Pinky Lee, Fred Flintstone, and "Star Trek."

A set of watch faces promoting the cartoon characters from the "Bullwinkle" series sells for $50. A boxed set of 6" vinyl figures from the same show is valued at $25. If "Bullwinkle" pleases you, then undoubtedly the Hanna-Barbera animated characters are of interest. Plastic and vinyl figural banks of Huckleberry Hound, Yogi Bear and Quick Draw McGraw made by Knickerbocker in the early 1970s can be purchased for $10 each. A rubber "squeak" toy of Fred Flintstone will cost you $6, while a pair of 4" "push-button puppets" of Fred Flintstone and Dino, made by Kohner in the 1960s, are selling for $15. The Hanna-Barbera Company (3400 Cahuenga Boulevard West, Hollywood, California 90068) continues to send out calendars and other similar items for promotional purposes. Because of the nature of this type of material and the groups to which it is sent, it could be that such items will be hard to find in years to come.

Corgi Toys in England makes die-cast models of cars featured in popular television series, such as Kojak's Buick ($10), the Saint's Jaguar ($8), Charlie's Angels' van ($9), and Starsky and Hutch's Ford ($10). Rag dolls of Redd Foxx as Fred Sanford sell for $6, while metal thermos bottles, manufactured by Thermos or Aladdin, are priced according to the popularity of the shows featured on the bottle: "Have Gun Will Travel" ($12), "The Beverly Hillbillies" ($10), "Get Smart" ($10), "Hogan's Heroes" ($10), "The Brady Bunch" ($5), "Hee-Haw" ($5), and "The Partridge Family" ($5).

From the golden age of television are Howdy Doody toys, such as a plastic take-apart puzzle and key chain ($8), a "Sun-Ray" plastic camera ($25), or a figural head cookie jar ($125). A Herb Shriner (remember him as television's answer to Will Rogers?) fan club membership kit, including a harmonica (which Shriner played when he wasn't dispensing homespun philosophy), sells for $10. Bozo the Clown items, such as a "soaky" bubble bath container, sell for between $5 and $10. A Pinky Lee wood and metal pull toy is valued at $22. My favorite item in the Lynn Becker catalogs is a 1952 pair of hand puppets of Danny O'Day and Humphrey Higsbye, the dummies used by ventriloquist Jimmy Nelson on "The Milton Berle Show." The puppets, marketed by Nelson's own company, are valued at $35.

Similar material is available from Hake's Americana and Collectibles of York, Pennsylvania. Hake's also features a considerable amount of paper collectibles in their catalogs. Here one may find comic books, coloring books, and games for cowboy heroes such as Gene Autry, Roy Rogers, the Lone Ranger, and Hopalong Cassidy, all of whom enjoyed earlier success on the screen and radio. Hake's sells only by auction, with each item given an approximate value. The prices realized generally seem to be above the values assigned. Its catalogs contain items on Tom Corbett, Space Cadet (such as an electronic inter-planet two-way phone, valued at $100), Batman (such as a Sears-Batman play set, valued at $125), and "Leave It to Beaver" (a "Leave It to Beaver" Rocket to the Moon Space Game, valued at $50). *TV Guides* can be found here, as well as an "I Love Lucy" doll ($100), *Burr Tillstrom's Kuklapolitan Courier Yearbook* ($50), and even paper dolls of Tabatha from "Bewitched" ($25). Hake's catalogs are available by subscription — $8 for four issues and $15 for eight issues. Hake's also publishes *Buttons in Sets, 1896-1972* by Marshall N. Levin and Theodore L. Hake. This reference guide covers promotional buttons in all fields, including radio and television. Did you know there was a set of buttons issued in connection with "Laugh In?" They are valued at between $6 and $8 each. Lynn Becker's catalogs sell for $2 each.

An assortment of early television novelty items. From left to right: set of five Howdy Doody finger puppets, $20; Howdy Doody key ring, $6. Howdy Doody bank, $65; Pinky Lee shoe laces, $5; Pinky Lee rubber doll, $25; a nightlight in the form of a television set, $25; Howdy Doody and Princess push puppets, $35 and $27.50; television salt and pepper shakers and a bank radio, $5 each.

A comic from the "Bewitched" series. $5.

Burr Tillstrom, Fran Allison, and the Kuklapolitan Players (Kukla, Ollie the Dragon, and company) remain perennial favorites for both children and adults.

A considerable number of television shows have also served as the basis for comic books. These include the Hanna-Barbera "Abbott and Costello" cartoon series (published in comic book form from 1968-1971), "Bat Masterson" (1959-1962), "Beany and Cecil" (1952-1963), "The Beverly Hillbillies" (1963-1971), "Bewitched" (1965-1969), "Bonanza" (1960-1970), "The Brady Bunch" (1970), "Bullwinkle" (1970-1971), "Burke's Law" (1964-1965), "The Cisco Kid" (1950-1958), "Colt .45" (1958-1961), "Daniel Boone" (1965-1969), "Dr. Kildare" (1962-1965), "The Flintstones" (1961-1979), "Get Smart" (1966-1967), "Gunsmoke" (1955-1961), "Happy Days" (1979-1980), "Howdy Doody" (1949-1956), "Huckleberry Hound" (1959-1978), "I Love Lucy" (1953-1962), "The Incredible Hulk" (1962 to present), "Laramie" (1960-1962), "Leave It to Beaver" (1958-1962), "The Man from U.N.C.L.E." (1965-1969), "Maverick" (1958-1962), "Mission Impossible" (1967-1969), "Mr. District Attorney" (1948-1959), "Mister Ed" (1962-1964), "My Little Margie" (1954-1964), "The Partridge Family" (1971-1973), "Rawhide" (1959-1962), "Sergeant Bilko" (1957-1960), "Sergeant Preston of the Yukon" (1951-1959), "77 Sunset Strip" (1960-1963), "The Twilight Zone" (1961-1982), "Voyage to the Bottom of the Sea" (1961-1970), "Yogi Bear" (1959-1979), and "Zorro" (1966-1968).

The definitive source for information relating to all types of comic books is *The Comic Book Price Guide* by Robert M. Overstreet and published by the author at 780 Hunt Cliff Drive NW, Cleveland, Tennessee 37311. The current edition is over four hundred pages in length and includes not only a detailed listing for every comic book title, but also lists of conventions, clubs, dealers, and useful articles. A valuable supplemental volume is Marcia Leiter's *Collecting Comic Books* (published by Little, Brown and Company, and available at any bookstore).

Comic book dealers are also useful sources for back issues of *TV Guide.* There are too many dealers (over five hundred) to list here. But I will recommend the American Comic Book Company (12206 Ventura Boulevard, P.O. Box 1809, Studio City, California 91604, (818) 763-8330). It publishes a comic book price list, which includes a separate section on movie and TV comics, listing 190 titles. There do not appear to be any clubs devoted solely to television comic books, and it lists only one fan publication, *The Adama Journal* (Silver Unicorn Graphics, P.O. Box 7000-822, Redondo Beach, California 90277) that is concerned solely with the comic-strip-style television series "Battlestar Galactica."

Thanks to the video revolution, most individuals wishing to own copies of their favorite television shows can simply tape them directly. They do not need to purchase tapes from the multitude of video cassette outlets that have sprung up across the country. Even so, it is worth bearing in mind that legitimate tapes available from legitimate dealers should be considerably superior to those made at home.

Although Thorne-EMI has started making available tapes of British television programs, there are still major gaps in what is available of the best of British television. Copies of "The Benny Hill Show" can be purchased, but "Doctor Who" cannot. The BBC has released videotapes in England of all episodes of the immensely popular (and very funny) "Fawlty Towers," starring John Cleese, but these are not, as yet, available in the United States. It is worth mentioning here that videotapes purchased in Europe *cannot* be played directly on American equipment without an expensive modification device. Such a machine became available for home use about a year ago at a cost of approximately $800. The trade name is Image Translator, and it can be used to play all PAL videotapes in color, including those from the Untied Kingdom, France, Australia, Scandinavia, South Africa, and South America, and all SECAM video tapes in monochrome, including those from Eastern Europe, the U.S.S.R., France, and the Middle East.

Former Warner Brothers cartoonist Bob Clampett came to television in the 1950s and 1960s with "Beany and Cecil."

Elizabeth Montgomery and Dick York starred in "Bewitched" (ABC, 1964-1972).

David McCallum, Robert Vaughn, and Leo G. Carroll on "The Man from U.N.C.L.E." (NBC, 1964-1968).

James Garner as "Maverick," seen on ABC from 1957-1960.

Ozzie, Harriet, Ricky, and David Nelson on "The Adventures of Ozzie and Harriet" (ABC, 1952-1966).

Filming a Kellogg's commercial in 1964 with Jimmy Durante. From left to right: Carl Hixon, Rudy Behlmer, Tom Armistead, and Jimmy Durante.

Most early television shows appear to be in the public domain, which means that any distributor lucky enough to acquire original material can offer videotape copies for sale. Unfortunately, it also means that one distributor can copy another distributor's tapes, resulting in a one-generation loss in picture and sound quality. Original material usually is in the form of a kinescope — a filmed record of 2 live television program often made for reference purposes only. Very few (sometimes only one) kinescopes were made of any particular program, so these 16mm films are highly sought after. If you are lucky, you may come across dealers at film conventions offering one or two, but in recent years those kinescopes still on the market have been limited to minor variety shows of the 1950s, such as the Los Angeles-produced "Polka Parade," which was actually syndicated around the country in kinescope rather than broadcast live. A few years ago it was possible to purchase 16mm kinescopic prints of "The Milton Berle Show" from the late 1940s and early 1950s for $50. Those days are long gone, and if one should come across such material today it would sell for close to $200 a show.

16mm prints of television series that were filmed in 35mm and distributed on film, such as "The Jack Benny Show," "The George Burns and Gracie Allen Show," and "The Adventures of Ozzie and Harriet" are frequently offered for sale at between $30 and $50 per show. Collectors can also find 16mm prints of television commercials for sale.

Highly prized are "classic" commercials, such as The Great American Soup commercial, featuring Ann Miller and produced by Stan Freberg. A highly desirable series of commercials are four from 1969 advertising Kellogg's Rice Krispies, produced by Rudy Behlmer and directed by Howard Morris. These commercials are parodies of "Maytime," "Il Pagliacci," "Carmen," and "Madame Butterfly," and were the first in a projected series. But as Rudy Behlmer recalls, "After receiving one letter in two thousand protesting our spoofing great music, there was some reluctance on the part of Kellogg's to continue."

Rudy Behlmer also directed two Buster Keaton commercials from 1964 promoting Pure Oil (now Union Oil) and a group of 1964-1965 Kellogg's Cornflakes commercials featuring Jimmy Durante. Behlmer should also receive credit for introducing the Pillsbury doughboy (who was later to become a corporate symbol) in 1966. Behlmer adds that all of these commercials were filmed in 35mm, with four prints made for network use. A contact 16mm negative was subsequently made, from which 16mm prints were made for general television use. It is these 16mm prints that can still be found.

Early television commercials can also provide fascinating but fleeting glimpses of today's stars in former reincarnations. Before Adam West became Batman, he was a television commercial father arguing the merits of Kellogg's Frosted Flakes and Black and Decker tools to his children. Jamie Farr, in his Before-"M*A*S*H" days, was the bullfighter singing a special version of the Toreador's Song from "Carmen" on the aforementioned Rice Krispies commercials. Some "stars" have never gone beyond the commercials stage of their careers. Jesse White is so much the Maytag repairman that no one remembers his earlier career as a dramatic actor. Virginia Christine will always be known as either the wife of character actor Fritz Feld or as Mrs. Olsen of Folger's coffee fame. There are probably more viewers today who remember Jane Withers as Josephine the Plumber than as a child star billed by Twentieth Century-Fox as the new Shirley Temple.

Despite the saturation level of commercial advertising on American television, photographs of the characters in such commercials are almost impossible to locate, and all are collector's items. As proof of the public's fascination with such items, 1985 saw the publication of *The TV Commercial Trivia Quiz Book* by Bruce Solomon and Michael Uslan (Priam, $6.95), who are also the authors of *The TV Trivia Quiz Book*.

The original 16mm prints of classic commercials are scarce. Prints of current television commercials have almost no value, as do 16mm prints of previews of new films, used for television advertising. These one- or two-minute reels should be available for little more than $1 each.

Many distributors offer videotapes of varying quality and prices on early television shows. Some have to be ordered directly, but most are available from any video outlet. Video Dimensions (110 East 23 Street, New York, New York 10010) has for sale videotapes from "You Asked for It" (with Art Baker), a 1965 "Dean Martin Show," a 1953 "Colgate Comedy Hour" with Eddie Cantor, a double bill of a 1953 "Carson's Cellar" (starring Johnny Carson before he took over "The Tonight Show") and a 1967 pilot for a Dick Cavett show titled "What's In." Also available from Video Dimensions is a 1949 "The Admiral Broadway Revue," featuring Sid Caesar and Imogene Coca; two 1966 episodes of "The Avengers," the popular British series starring Patrick MacNee and Diana Rigg; a "Bulova Watch Time" show from 1951 starring Frank Sinatra; a 1956 "Perry Como Show;" and a selection of television bloopers.

"Amos 'n' Andy" was one of the most popular shows on CBS from 1951-1953. It starred Alvin Childress as Amos and Spencer Williams as Andy. Because of concerns over racial stereotypes, the series has never been revived — despite pressure from fans. Because it cannot be seen on television, videotapes of the shows are highly sought after. At one time, only one or two videotapes were available, but times have changed. Cumberland Video (Suite 104, 3917 West Riverside Drive, Burbank, California 91505) has over fifty episodes available. Foothill Video (7730 Foothill Boulevard, Tujunga, California 91409) has forty episodes for sale. Shokus Video (P.O. Box 8434, Van Nuys, California 91409) offers twenty-four episodes. Shokus also sells a 1949 Ed Wynn show, episodes of "The Toast of the Town" from 1954 and 1956, a 1956 "Walter Winchell Show," a 1958 "Person to Person" on which Edward R. Murrow's guest was Groucho Marx, eight episodes from "The Adventures of Ozzie and Harriet," and two separate selections of vintage commercials. In December 1984, National Telefilm Associates, a major distributor of films and shows to television, announced that it was offering a single videocassette of three "Amos 'n' Andy" shows for $19.95. NTA's tapes are available from any

Rudy Behlmer (left) with television's best-known repairman, Jesse White, representing Maytag.

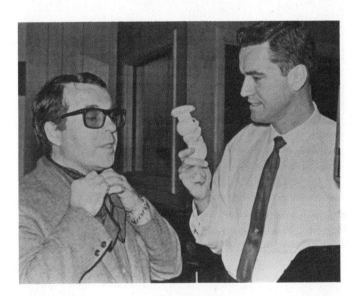

Rudy Behlmer (right) with one of television's most active commercial voice-overs, Paul Frees, and the Pillsbury Doughboy, whom Behlmer introduced to television.

In 1956, one of Ed Sullivan's guests was British revue star Joyce Grenfell.

Groucho Marx with his announcer George Fenneman on "The Best of Groucho," also known as "You Bet Your Life" (NBC, 1950-1961).

outlet, and the company is worth watching as it may offer videotapes of other shows to which it controls rights, such as the 1959-1962 series of "The Third Man," starring Michael Rennie.

Eddie Brandt is a recommended source for videotapes from any dealer. Among the classic TV shows available on video from his company are three videotapes of Elvis Presley, the Mack Sennett episode of "This Is Your Life," an hour-long sample of Ernie Kovacs titled "Best of Ernie Kovacs," two "Howdy Doody" shows, Roy Acuff's "Open House" Volumes 1 and 2, and episodes from "Mama," "The Jack Benny Show," "My Little Margie," "Flash Gordon" (featuring Steve Holland), and "You Bet Your Life."

Video Images (465 Monroe Turnpike, Monroe, Connecticut 06468) offers a major selection under the heading of "The Golden Age of Television." Included are the extremely rare "I Married Joan" shows, featuring Joan Davis and Jim Backus; "The Original Amateur Hour," with Ted Mack; "Hullabaloo;" "Life Is Worth Living," with Bishop Fulton J. Sheen, who is surely, aside from Liberace, the most "camp" individual ever to star on network television; "The Colgate Comedy Hour;" "Mama;" "Rocky Jones, Space Ranger;" "The Dinah Shore Show;" "The Arthur Godfrey Show;" "The Quiz Kids;" "Dr. I.Q.;" and many more. Video Images, whose quality is usually good, and which is one of the few companies to indicate when a particular tape is not up to acceptable standards, also offers many "specials." These include "Summer in New York" with Phil Silvers; "Elvis — Aloha from Hawaii" via satellite; "Judy and Her Guests," with Judy Garland and Robert Goulet; "Ford Star Jubilee," with Noel Coward and Mary Martin; "The Fabulous Fred Astaire;" and the Twenty-seventh annual Academy Awards presentation (1955). Also available are episodes from dramatic programs such as "Studio One," "Goodyear TV Playhouse," "Playwrights '56," and "Hallmark Theater."

Penguin Video (Box 65156, Los Angeles, California 90065) is another good source for vintage television, with some material also available in the form of 16mm prints. There are episodes of "The Abbott and Costello Show," "Amos 'n' Andy," "The Avengers," "My Little Margie," "The Adventures of Ozzie and Harriet," "Flash Gordon," and "The Milton Berle Show." Penguin also offers a 1959 thirty-minute unsold pilot, "The Left Fist of David," directed by Buzz Kulik and starring Vincent Price and Peter Lorrie.

The best source of information on video equipment and videotape or disc collecting remains *The Complete Guide to Home Video* by Leonard Maltin and Allan Greenfield, published in 1981 by Harmony Books. It needs updating, but it is still reliable. The best source for current information on new releases on video (and, for that matter, all aspects of video-recording) is *Video Review* (325 East 75 Street, New York, New York 10021). Other video journals include *Home Video* (475 Park Avenue South, New York, New York 10016), *The Videophile* (2003 Apalachee Parkway, Tallahassee, Florida 32301), *Videography* (750 Third Avenue, New York, New York 10017), *Video News* (8401 Connecticut Avenue, Washington, D.C. 20015), and *Video Movies Magazine* (3841 West Oakton Street, Skokie, Illinois 60076).

To find out what is available on video, the best single source is possibly *The Video Source Book*, published by the National Video Clearinghouse. It costs $125. There is also a British edition available — just to make your mouth water at what is unavailable over here. The National Video Clearinghouse also publishes *The Video Tape & Disc Guide to Home Entertainment* in a paperback edition. Also recommended is *Videolog: Programs for General Interest and Entertainment* available in paperback from Video-Forum (96 Broad Street, Guilford, Connecticut 06437). Videolog also has available volumes devoted to General Interest and Education, Business, and Health Sciences. As proof of the strength of the video revolution, there are 121 books beginning with the word "video" listed in the 1983-1984 edition of *Books in Print*.

For anyone interested in collecting classic films *and* classic television, the best sources of information are two newspaper-style periodicals, which are full of news, gossip, advertising, and articles of varying degrees of accuracy and intelligence. They are *Classic Images* (P.O. Box 809, Muscatine, Iowa 52761) and *The Big Reel* (Route 3, Madison, North Carolina 27025). Twelve issues of *Classic Images* cost $20 by second-class mail; twelve issues of *The Big Reel* are available for $15.

General information as to who distributes what on television is provided by the Broadcast Information Bureau, commonly known as BIB, a division of the National Video Clearinghouse. BIB publishes the *TV Feature Film Source Book*, which lists available features and their distributors. It seems as if almost every sound feature film is in television distribution, but as far as many film buffs are concerned, the problem is that television stations are simply unwilling to program black-and-white films during prime-time viewing hours. Also available from BIB is *Series, Serials & Packages*, which provides useful information about programs now in syndication, including descriptions, dates of first and last network showings, and running times.

There is no adequate documentation or information on the satisfactory storage of precious videotapes. Experts generally agree that the tapes should be stored standing (as books are shelved) at room temperature and low humidity. The theory that videotapes should be stored at a cold temperature has now been dismissed. No one knows for sure for how long a videotape will retain its image and sound. Some videotapes are of better quality than others, but occasionally tapes from a highly reputable manufacturer can be faulty. Tapes can last as long as twenty-five years and as few as five. The only way to ensure their preservation is to make new copies, which, of course, results in a slight loss of quality. Running a tape at least once a year will not ensure longer life, but is possible that storing the tapes with the tails out, rather than rewinding them after each viewing, will help to preserve the image a little longer.

Because the video revolution is still in progress, tapes made on obsolete machines utilizing defunct systems may be lost forever unless archival institutions can retain at least one example of every tape recorder manufactured. No one really knows what the future holds, but it could be that Beta, VHS, or video discs will eventually become outmoded. And once the current machines have ceased to function, new models will not be available to play the tapes recorded upon them. Perhaps videotape will prove to be as transitory as television itself.

There are a number of institutions offering facilities for viewing early television programs, but the majority of them are usually only accessible to bona fide researchers. Television news may, at first glance, appear to have only immediate interest, but a study of news programming through the years can provide scholars with an understanding of the political and popular climate prevalent in the country during a particular period, as well as suggest biases in the ways in which the news has been reported. For example, would the American people have expressed such major opposition to the war in Vietnam if the news media hadn't presented that war from a liberal viewpoint? Similarly, would Americans have accepted quite as easily the deposing of the Shah of Iran had CBS' "60 Minutes" not been so enthusiastic in its reporting of the atrocities committed in his name?

The best-known ABC news anchormen, Howard K. Smith and Harry Reasoner.

57

Edward R. Murrow's "Person to Person" was a television high spot from 1953 to 1959.

Joan Davis and Jim Backus on "I Married Joan" (NBC, 1952-1955).

When Nashville businessman Paul C. Simpson discovered that the networks were not retaining their nightly news broadcasts, he decided to ensure that such valuable records of our times would be preserved. During 1968, Simpson videotaped the presidential campaign as reported by the news media. His videotapes demonstrated the importance of such documentary coverage. Two years later, Simpson was able to gain financial support for his work from two Nashville foundations, and in 1971 the Vanderbilt Television News Archive came into being on the campus of Nashville's Vanderbilt University.

Despite opposition and, indeed, a lawsuit from the networks, Vanderbilt has taped and preserved the ABC, CBS, and NBC evening news broadcasts from August 5, 1968, to the present. It also tapes political events, presidential speeches, and Senate and House hearings (such as those on Watergate). The tapes are indexed by subject and can be duplicated for loan purposes. The Archive has also published the *Television News Index and Abstract* since August 1968. The Vanderbilt Television News Archive is open to the public by appointment. Researchers should write to the Archive at 419 21st Avenue South, Nashville, Tennessee 37203.

As a result of the Vanderbilt activities, the National Archives in Washington, D.C. has also commenced taping the network evening news programs. Also in Washington, D.C., is housed the Television News Study Center of George Washington University (2130 H Street NW, Washington, D.C. 20052). The Center has published *Television Network News: Issues in Content Research,* edited by William Adams and Fay Schreibman in 1978. This publication provides a guide to television news archives. CBS is the only network that publishes an index to its news broadcasts. The index is available at most major libraries.

The Library of Congress (Washington, D.C. 20540) is quick to note that its holdings of early television shows are not major, although the Library does have a fine collection on "The Original Amateur Hour," featuring Ted Mack. The Library did inaugurate a series of lunch-time screenings of television shows during 1984. Each show was screened four times a day to enthusiastic audiences. "Tell It to Groucho," "The Phil Silvers Show," and "The Jack Benny Show" proved to be the most popular attractions. TV programs are also screened occasionally during the Library's evening shows, but as programmer Scott Simmons points out, "Unfortunately, television is not as popular in the evening as film, because people seem to question why they should go out to see something that they can see at home with the turn of a switch."

The largest television archives in the western United States is the ATAS-UCLA Television Archives. Part of the UCLA Film, Television and Radio Archives, it is associated with the Academy of Television Arts and Sciences. Archivist Dan Einstein says of the collection, "As far as the items go, there are approximately twenty thousand, a lot of which are negatives, duplicate copies, and bits and pieces of things. As far as complete viewable programs, there are probably about ten thousand. The earliest item is a presentation, a sales reel

John Chancellor and David Brinkley cover the Democratic National Convention for NBC in 1980.

for NBC from 1946, and we have a few things from 1947 and 1948." In terms of complete shows, the Archives includes almost all the "Hallmark" shows and about 75 percent of "The Jack Benny Shows." Also in the collection are "Alcoa Theatre," "Alcoa Hour," "Alcoa Premiere," "The Loretta Young Show," "Ann Sothern Show," and "Joey Bishop Show." Steve Allen's syndicated TV shows from the early 1960s are available, and the Archives is in the process of acquiring "Mannix" and "Mork and Mindy" from Paramount. The first five hundred shows of "Entertainment Tonight" and 250 originally produced shows from Home Box Office are also on record. Because the Archives is associated with the Television Academy, it gets many of the Emmy nominees and winners, but fewer news and documentary shows.

UCLA also holds shows featuring Milton Berle, Ernie Kovacs, the Smothers Brothers, Dick Van Dyke, Lucille Ball, Ozzie and Harriet Nelson, and many other personalities. Among the early television items in the collection (usually on film) are a 1931 Paramount newsreel, in which Rudy Vallee explains mechanical television; a Movietone News presentation of the 1936 opening of the BBC's Alexander Palace studio; John Logie Baird in 1938 describing television apparatus at London's Science Museum; a 1939 *Popular Science* subject featuring television pioneer Philo T.

Farnsworth; and Emperor Hirohito of Japan viewing a television demonstration in Tokyo in 1949. A useful catalog of the Archives' holdings was published in 1981 by Redgrave Publishing (430 Manville Road, Pleasantville, New York 10570), but it is now considerably out-of-date.

In addition to the programs themselves, UCLA's Theatre Arts Library has television-related paper material, including the collections of Jack Benny, Eddie Cantor, Ernie Kovacs, Gene Roddenberry (and his complete files for "Star Trek"), Rod Serling, and the Smothers Brothers. The Theatre Arts Library also possesses a large collection of television scripts, including those for "Matinee Theatre," "The Further Adventures of Ellery Queen," and "I Spy." Across town, the Special Collections Department of the Doheny Memorial Library at the University of Southern California has the papers of Steve Allen, George Burns, Chuck Connors, Freeman Gosden, and Charlie Correll, as well as a large television script collection.

The ATAS-UCLA collection is open for viewing, but it is necessary to make an appointment at least seven days in advance. Except for people involved in a major research project, viewings are limited to three hours per quarter. Original kinescopes can no longer be viewed, but taped copies are generally available.

The entrance to New York's Museum of Broadcasting.

Dick Van Dyke and Mary Tyler Moore on "The Dick Van Dyke Show" (CBS, 1961-1966).

Perry Como's Christmas specials are a popular television perennial. Here he is seen in 1983 with "Perry Como's Christmas in New York."

The Wisconsin Center for Film and Theatre Research (816 State Street, Madison, Wisconsin 53706) holds the papers for a number of people, in the television industry, including Alan Alda, Paddy Chayefsky, Fred Coe, and John Frankenheimer. Because it has the United Artists Collection, Wisconsin also holds 16mm prints from many of the Ziv Television productions (purchased by United Artists in 1960), including "Boston Blackie" (1951-1953), "The Cisco Kid" (1950-1956), "Highway Patrol" (1955-1959), and "Mr. District Attorney" (1951-1952). The Ziv Archives is housed in the Division of Broadcasting at the University of Cincinnati.

On the East Coast, the Department of Manuscripts and Special Collections of Syracuse University Library (Syracuse, New York 13210) has the papers of Mike Wallace and Gertrude Berg, as well as the correspondence files of *Television Quarterly*.

In New York City, the Museum of Modern Art has some television holdings, with its first acquisition having been the March 1, 1953, Philco Playhouse presentation of "The Trip to Bountiful," produced by Fred Coe, written by Horton Foote, and starring Lillian Gish and Eva Marie Saint. Recently the musuem has recognized the work of video artists, but those who recognize video as an artform are seldom those whose video works are seen on television. The museum's film and video collections are accessible to bona fide researchers only, and there is a fee.

The Television Information Office (TIO) was founded in October 1959 as "a two-way bridge of understanding between the television industry and its many publics." It maintains what is claimed to be "the nation's most extensive information center and library specializing in the social, cultural, and programming aspects of television." It receives more than two hundred periodicals annually, maintains clippings files, and offers special services to the press, broadcasters, and educators. TIO publishes the biannual *Teachers' Guides to Television* and offers a series of half-hour programs, titled "Television in America," as well as slide presentations.

Students study television at the Museum of Broadcasting's video consoles.

Available from TIO is a listing of Periodicals in Broadcasting and Communications, as well as a list of publications, among which are *ABCs of Radio and Television, The Shaping of the Television Medium, The Black Image on TV, Commercial Television as a Teaching Tool,* and *Careers in Television.* All TIO publications cost just a few cents and are available in bulk for teaching purposes.

The only subject-oriented broadcast archives in the country is the National Jewish Archive of Broadcasting at the Jewish Museum (1109 Fifth Avenue, New York, New York 10128). Launched in 1981 with a grant from the Charles H. Revson Foundation, the National Jewish Archive of Broadcasting is concerned with the acquisition, preservation, and cataloging of news, public affairs, religious, and entertainment programs whose subject matter is of interest to the Jewish community. To date, the Archive has more than six hundred programs, along with a library of press releases, clippings, and reference books. The material is accessible to bona fide researchers only. The Archive also presents public screenings and lectures at the Jewish Museum under the general title of "An Invitation To Watch TV at Our House."

The programs in the Archive's collection vary from documentary footage, such as "Golda Meir Address" (1970) and "Eternal Light — A Conversation with Isaac Bashevis Singer" (1966) to "You Are There — The Plot against King Solomon" (1954) and, of course, Gertrude Berg's brilliant radio and television series, "The Goldbergs."

The most prestigious organization concerned with the preservation of television is the Museum of Broadcasting, founded in 1976 by William S. Paley (founding chairman of CBS). The museum houses what is possibly the nation's largest archives of quality radio and television programs from all three networks. "It is a small museum, quiet and orderly," wrote Richard F. Shepard in *The New York Times* (July 13, 1980), "yet, when one puts on the headphones at a console, the passions and frivolities of the century greet the eyes and ears." Included in the museum's collection is a segment from a 1939 NBC television drama, "The Streets of New York," and just about everything one would expect from the golden age of television. In 1981, Arno Press published the now out-of-date *The Catalog of the Museum of Broadcasting: The History of American Broadcasting as Documented by the Programs in the Radio and Television Collection.*

The museum's own building includes a sixty-three-seat threatre equipped with a video projector. Here are presented special series, such as salutes to Bob and Ray, the Muppets, Telefis Eireann, the BBC, and Sid Caesar. There is also an informal viewing room on the second floor, with seating for twenty. Twenty-three television consoles are available for individual viewing. Time at the consoles is limited to one hour for the general public, but members can reserve space in advance. There is a nominal charge. The museum also has a small, but growing, library of books and periodicals on the history of broadcasting, a radio script collection, and the NBC Radio Archive, consisting of 175,000 historic discs.

On June 26, 1955, the seventh anniversary of "Toast of the Town," Ed Sullivan welcomed Sullivan impersonator Will Jordan (left).

More than ten thousand videotapes are held by the museum, with the most popular being the 1964 appearance by the Beatles on the "Ed Sullivan Show." The choice of programs by clients upsets the museum's staff, according to a June 3, 1982, article in *The Wall Street Journal.* This illustrates the fact that those involved in television scholarship are out of touch with what television is all about and why it has survived in popularity. It is not surprising that Alistair Cooke has been asked to give his seal of approval to the museum's operation in a pamphlet titled *The Museum of Broadcasting: A Personal View.* One of these days, a television institution will have the courage to publish a personal view by Penny Marshall or Lawrence Welk.

Membership in the Museum of Broadcasting includes complimentary admission to the museum's programs, a subscription to *MB News,* use of a telephone reference service, and reserved use of the radio and television consoles. In recent years, the museum has initiated a traveling program of the best of early television, but the quality of the tapes in the program suggests that the golden age of television was more the age of soot and whitewash. The museum would do well to try to improve its tapes, which do a decided disservice to television history.

Concern with television's past is not limited solely to American organizations. In London, the National Film Archive, a division of the British Film Institute (81 Dean Street, London WIV 6AA) has preserved a considerable number of British and American television programs. In 1981, it published *Keeping Television Alive: The Television Work of the National Film Archive.* The International Federation of Film Archives has recognized the importance of television and now publishes an *International Index to Television Periodicals.*

Art Baker with knife-throwing expert Auggie Gomez on "You Asked for It," first televised in 1950.

"The Red Skelton Show" was broadcast from 1951-1971. Here Skelton's guest is Jerry Lewis.

A SKYE PUBLICATIO

TV

25c
•
JANUARY
•
ANC

The Loves in their Lives!

FISHER

SINATRA

LIBERACE

WEBB

Stories and Pictures of Your TV Favorites

TV, **January 1955. $10.**

TV Fan, December 1955. $10.

Eddie Fisher: Heading For A Breakdown?

NOV. 25c

TV HEADLINER

THE MAGAZINE OF TELEVISION EXCLUSIVES

TV HEADLINER

■

The Inside Story:

IS LIBERACE SLIPPING?

■

LORETTA YOUNG Gives You A "Faith For Every Day"

■

The Truth About THOSE TV TABOOS!

■

EXCLUSIVE PIX! UNDERGROUND WITH ART CARNEY!

ALSO
Dorothy Collins
Judy Holliday
Robert Cummings
George Gobel

Steve Allen: Happy or Henpecked?

TV Headliner, November 1955. $10.

A souvenir handed out to members of the audiences at tapings of "The Lawrence Welk Show."

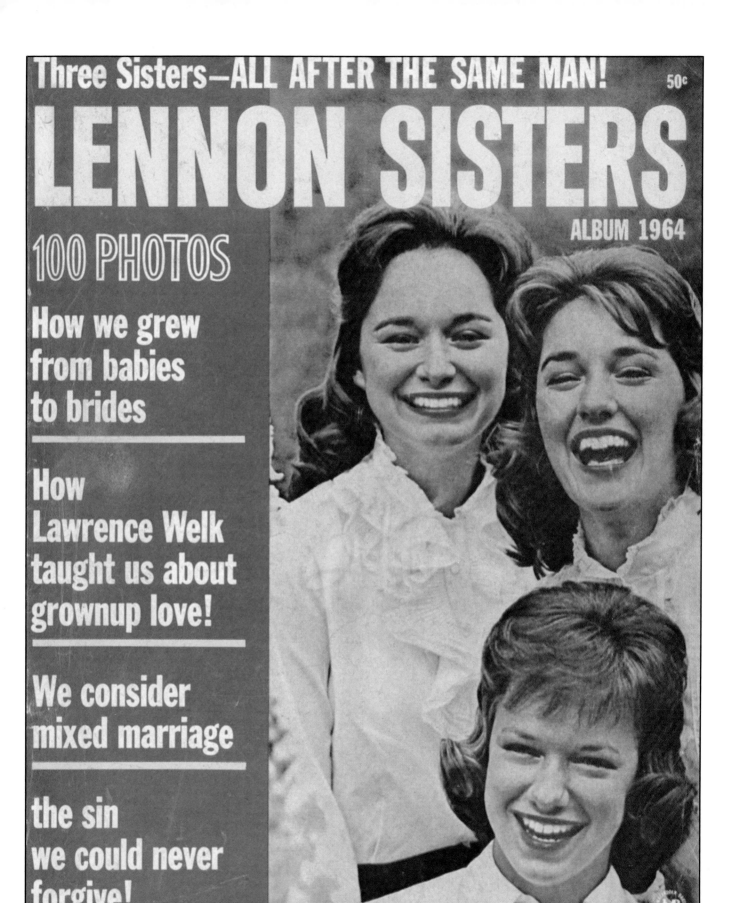

Lennon Sisters Album from 1964. $9.

One of "The Man from U.N.C.L.E." comics. $7.

I Love Lucy with a delightful cover. $6.

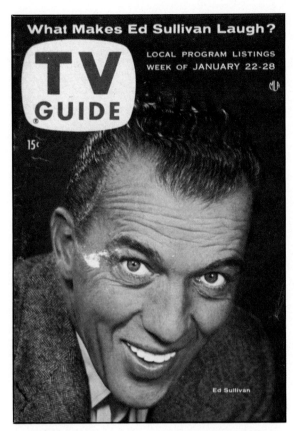

TV Guide for the week of January 22 to 28, 1955. $5.

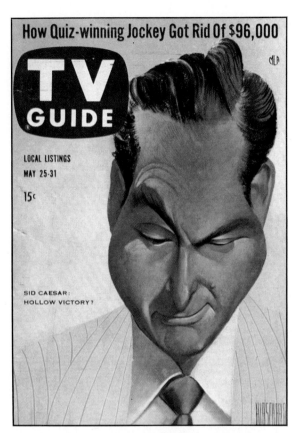

TV Guide for the week of May 25 to 31, 1957. $5.

An original 1957 Pocket Book edition of Earl Wilson's *The NBC Book of Stars*. $10.

The series was officially known as "You'll Never Get Rich" or "The Phil Silvers Show," but everyone knew it as "Sergeant Bilko." It was created by Nat Hiken and seen on CBS from 1955-1959.

Program for a 1962 television series at New York's Museum of Modern Art. $10.

Jerome Cowan was a guest on the January 16, 1961, episode of "The Danny Thomas Show" (CBS).

Shirley Booth starred as "Hazel," the housekeeper, on NBC and CBS from 1961-1966.

Richard Simmons as "Sergeant Preston of the Yukon" (CBS, 1955-1958).

Former silent star Esther Ralston, featured on the soap opera "Our Five Daughters."

Bob Crane, surrounded by some of the memorabilia created by his popular 1965-1971 CBS series, "Hogan's Heroes."

"The Munsters," better known to their friends as (from left to right) Butch Patrick, Al Lewis, Fred Gwynne, Yvonne DeCarlo, and Pat Priest (CBS, 1964-1966).

"The Munsters" had competition on ABC (1964-1966) from "The Addams Family," based on characters created by *The New Yorker* cartoonist Charles Addams. Carolyn Jones played Morticia, John Astin was Gomez, and Jackie Coogan was Uncle Fester.

A comic for the 1967-1968 ABC series "Garrison's Gorillas," — starring Ron Harper. $2.

Richard Greene in the title role from "The Adventures of Robin Hood" (1955-1958).

One of a series of books chronicling the adventures of "The Man from U.N.C.L.E.," and published by Ace Books. This volume from 1965 is valued at $5.

Lorne Greene, Pernell Roberts, Dan Blocker, and Michael Landon on "Bonanza," as the Cartwrights, a family that made its NBC debut in 1959.

77 SUNSET STRIP

149 hours of sophisticated adventure

An unusually popular cast of crisply drawn characters with enduring appeal form the nucleus of 77 SUNSET STRIP — the glamorous address of a highly successful and daring young pair of investigators who have formed their own agency.

Stu Bailey, a former OSS officer (played by Efrem Zimbalist, Jr.) and his partner Jeff Spencer (Roger Smith) manage to attract a variety of clients whose problems often require fast trips to the far corners of the globe. "Kookie" (Ed Byrnes) is the hair-combing, hip-talking parking lot attendant at Dino's restaurant, who frequently gets involved in the exciting adventures of Bailey and Spencer. "Kookie" eventually graduates to a full-time partnership.

WARNER BROS.-SEVEN ARTS
NEW YORK: 200 Park Ave. • (212) 986-1717
CHICAGO: 550 West Jackson Blvd. • (312) 372-8089
DALLAS: 508 Park Ave. • (214) 747-9925
LOS ANGELES: 291 S. La Cienega Blvd., Beverly Hills • (213) 657-1771
TORONTO, ONTARIO: 11 Adelaide St. West • (416) 364-7193
LONDON • SYDNEY • TOKYO • MEXICO CITY • NASSAU

SUGARFOOT

69 hours of fast-moving western action

A different kind of Western hero, whose saddle bags are crammed with correspondence school law books — that's lanky Tom Brewster ("SUGARFOOT") played by Will Hutchins.

Idealistic and romantic — but nobody's fool — he can ride a horse and use a gun, knife, or rope with the best of them. Fast-thinking, peace-loving — a man who'd rather talk things out than resort to force — SUGARFOOT has all the ingredients of a western favorite with mass appeal.

WARNER BROS.-SEVEN ARTS
NEW YORK: 700 Park Ave. • (212) 986-1717
CHICAGO: 550 West Jackson Blvd. • (312) 372-8089
DALLAS: 508 Park Ave. • (214) 747-9925
LOS ANGELES: 291 S. La Cienega Blvd., Beverly Hills • (213) 657-1771
TORONTO, ONTARIO: 11 Adelaide St. West • (416) 364-7193
LONDON • SYDNEY • TOKYO • MEXICO CITY • NASSAU

When television programs are cancelled and go into syndicated release, their distributors sell them to television stations, utilizing advertising matter such as this, valued at $1 per page.

Buddy Ebsen teaches tap dancing to Lee Meriwether on "Barnaby Jones" (CBS, 1973-1980).

On the May 19, 1974, episode of "McMillan & Wife," Dana Wynter and Steve Forrest were featured with star Rock Hudson.

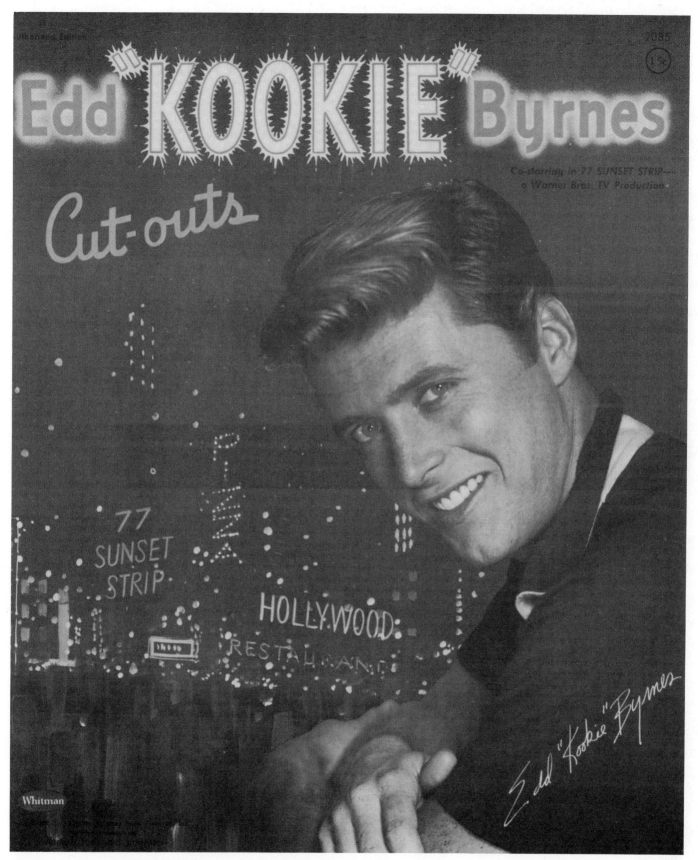

Whitman published this Edd "Kookie" Byrnes cut-out book in 1959. It is now valued at $25. Byrnes was featured from 1958-1963 on the popular ABC series, "77 Sunset Strip."

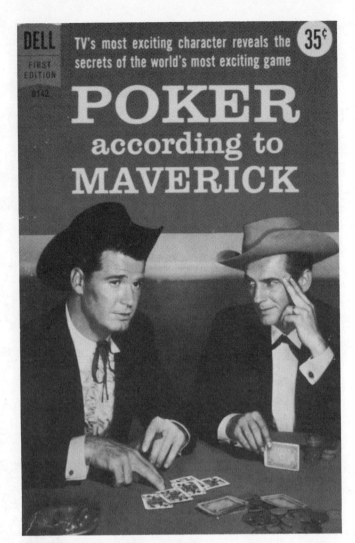

A textbook on poker, published in 1959 by Dell in connection with the 1957-1962 series "Maverick." James Garner and Jack Kelly are featured on the cover. $10.

Even "Burke's Law" (ABC, 1963-1966) generated a paperback book series. This one, from England, was published by Fontana in 1964 and is valued at $4.

A 1969 Whitman book based on the 1967-1975 series "Ironside," starring Raymond Burr. $5.

Patrick McGoohan was "The Prisoner," a British television series seen on CBS from 1968-1969.

"Sanford and Son" was based on a popular BBC series, "Steptoe and Son," with Wilfrid Brambell as the father and Harry H. Corbett as the son.

Redd Foxx and Demond Wilson were the stars of "Sanford and Son" (NBC, 1972-1976).

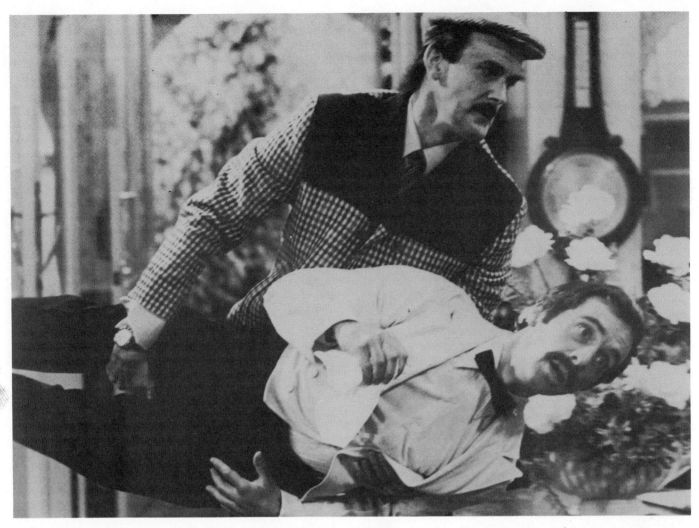

John Cleese as Basil Fawlty and Andrew Sachs as Manuel on "Fawlty Towers," the BBC series to be seen on PBS.

Claire Bloom as Lady Marchmain and Jeremey Irons as Charles Ryder from the most popular series on PBS, "Brideshead Revisited." The first episode was televised Monday, January 18, 1982.

The most popular British series to be seen on American television was, unquestionably, "Monty Python's Flying Circus."

The theme music for "Dragnet," published in 1953. $6.

Here he is: Bert Parks with the 1969 winner of the Miss America title, Judith Anne Ford.

Carol Burnett and Jesse White were featured in "Cavender Is Coming," a 1962 episode of "The Twilight Zone."

"Amahl and the Night Visitors" by Gian-Carlo Menotti was the first opera to be commissioned for television. It has been televised regularly by NBC since 1951. Menotti is seen here with Teresa Stratas, who played the mother.

Two ladies who are equally at home as entertainers and talk show hosts, Dinah Shore and Joan Rivers.

Carol Burnett with Vicki Lawrence, who was a regular during the entire run of "The Carol Burnett Show" on CBS and ABC from 1967-1979.

Tony Randall and Jack Klugman were "The Odd Couple" on ABC from 1970-1975.

"Charlie's Angels," from 1976-1977, were Jaclyn Smith, Kate Jackson, and Farrah Fawcett-Majors.

Tony Curtis was one of the guest stars on "Rowan & Martin's Laugh-In" (NBC, 1968-1973). He is seen here with regulars Chelsea Brown, Jo Anne Worley, Goldie Hawn, Ruth Buzzi, and Judy Carne.

Two popular television stars in their own right, Paul Lynde and Totie Fields guest-starred on a 1969 episode of "The Jerry Lewis Show."

Ricardo Montalban with his original co-star, Herve Villechaize, on "Fantasy Island," seen on ABC from 1978-1984.

An autographed photograph of the original stars of ABC's "The Love Boat," first televised in 1977. $15.

"The Beverly Hillbillies" welcome Phil Silvers. From left to right: Buddy Ebsen, Irene Ryan, Phil Silvers, Max Baer, Jr., and Donna Douglas. "The Beverly Hillbillies" was seen on CBS from 1962-1971.

"My Favorite Martian" was Ray Walston (CBS, 1963-1966).

Captain Kangaroo, joined in 1978 by John Burstein in "The Adventures of Slim Goodbody" (who, this being children's television, does not appear to have any sex organs).

An assortment of dolls based on television characters. From left to right: Mork (Robin Williams) talking rag doll, $10; Mork talking back-pack doll, $7; "Welcome Back, Kotter" dolls, $8. each; a Monkees talking hand puppet, $15; and a Flip Wilson doll from 1970, which turns around to become "Geraldine," $12.

A rare photograph from KLAC-TV in Los Angeles, 1951. Rudy Behlmer is cupping his hand to his mouth; at far right is Jim Hobson, who became director of "The Lawrence Welk Show;" and seated alone in the first row is none other than director-to-be Sam Peckinpah.

Filming a Buster Keaton commercial for Pure Oil in 1964.

3
The Equipment

In 1979, *TV Guide* announced that collecting TV receivers was "a hot new trend." The market for post-war 7 inch and 10 inch sets has increased in recent years, with most receivers from the later 1940s now selling for approximately $75 each. Particularly popular with both collectors and trendsetters who find a fascination with anything of the 1950s is the Philco Predicta set, which has a plastic shield in the shape of a picture tube on top.

Television sets that date to the early days of television are expensive and hard to locate. They can sell for between $3,000 and $5,000 each. One exceptionally rare and eagerly sought item is the RCA RR-359 Field Test Receiver, dating from 1936-1938. One hundred experimental models were built and then loaned to NBC and RCA engineers and executives. The RCA TRK-12 Mirror-Lid receiver from 1939 is also rare. It originally sold for $600 and required the viewer to watch the television picture in a mirror placed inside the lid. It was housed in an extremely attractive art deco case designed by John Vassos, who was considered America's foremost industrial designer.

Impossible to locate are pre-1939 television cameras. The networks did not keep them, institutions do not have them in their archives, and none are known to exist in private collections. Indeed, there are exceedingly few surviving items of equipment relating to the historical development of television. Only two of CBS' Field Sequential Color System television receivers from 1951 are known to be extant. One is owned by a collector, Arnold Chase, in Connecticut, and the other by Los Angeles collector Ed Reitan, who has turned down offers of up to $10,000 for some of his early television experimental equipment.

Ed Reitan is the guiding force behind the Collection of Television Technology and Design, which is maintained by the ATAS-UCLA Archives. Among the holdings of UCLA are a Western Television Corporation "Visionette" Televisor from 1930, an example of mechanical television; the Don Lee Experimental Receiver from 1937; the RCA Victor 630TS from 1946, which Reitan regards as "the most influential receiver produced;" the RCA Triniscope Color Receiver from 1950; an RCA TK-10 Studio Camera from 1946; an RCA TK-41 NTSC Color Camera from 1954; and the GPL Kinescope Recorder, dating from around 1953. The UCLA collection is not presently available for viewing, but it is described in great detail in Reitan's paper, "Preserving the History of Television at UCLA: The Collection of Television Technology and Design," in *IEEE Transactions on Consumer Electronics,* Vol. CE-30, No. 2, May 1984.

The ATAS-UCLA priorities for collection, restoration and preservation include:

Black-and-white television system development (RCA, Farnsworth, Philco, Dumont, Hazeltine, and original NTSC).

Color television system development (CBS, RCA, CTI, and second NTSC).

Live and film pick-up camera and broadcast equipment development (iconoscope, dissector, orthicon, image orthicon, plumbicon, and ENG).

Receiver development (mechanical scanning, electronic pre- and post-war, color, projection).

Video recording systems (kinescope film recording, magnetic video, transverse and helical, video disc).

Industrial design (identification of innovations in design and styling).

The Archive is also eager to acquire historical documentation, incuding manuals, drawings, technical reports, texts, and oral histories from film pioneers. Currently, there is little interest in such documentation among collectors. Most major public libraries have a good collection of television manuals, both past and present.

The ATAS-UCLA collection is possibly the finest institutional collection of its type. There are other collections of television-related materials at the Smithsonian Institution in Washington, D.C., and at the Los Angeles County Museum of Natural History.

According to Ed Reitan, "Most television-related collecting is derivative from radio collecting, which is far more rampant. And strangely, most radio equipment collectors are disdainful of television." One of the few sources for early television receivers is, in fact, a shop that specializes primarily in early radios, phonographs and 78 r.p.m. records. It is called Waves (32 East 13 Street, New York, New York 10003).

A newsletter for collectors of television receivers is published by Ken McIntosh (907 Radcliff, Baltimore, Maryland 21204), who has a fine collection relating to mechanical television. "Mechanical television," was the earliest form of television, as demonstrated by C. Francis Jenkins in the United States and John Logie Baird in the United Kingdom. It was based on a scanning disc, invented in 1884 by Paul Nipkow, which illustrates just how old is the theory of television. It was fairly primitive and was quickly superceded by electronic television.

Typical of the collectors of television receivers is Charles Murray of Los Angeles, who owns approximately two hundred pre-1950 sets. He became interested in the hobby after acquiring a set inexpensively at a garage sale. Murray points out that collecting television equipment is still the hobby of only a few individuals, all of whom tend to know each other. It is also a field in which prices have not stabilized. Some 1949 sets sold for $150 in 1984, but were selling for less than $80 a year later when householders began digging them out of basements and garages and swamped the market. Oddball, custom-built sets, however, generally increase in value.

Although there are no specific outlets for television receivers, collectors may start looking at local television repair shops, many of which may have retained one or two models from the past. In Los Angeles, one establishment that offers early receivers for sale is Bill Saul's Hollywood TV (5622 Lankershim Boulevard, North Hollywood, California 91602).

Garage sales can still yield bargains for collectors of television receivers. One of the best-known private collections was that of costume designer Kent Warner. It was featured in *Collectibles Illustrated, TV Guide*, and many other publications. Warner owned a 1939 Dumont, a 1960 Philco Predicta, and an RCA TRK-12, which was supposedly the original demonstration model used at the 1939 World's Fair. Kent Warner died in 1983, and rumor has it that the bulk of his collection was sold by his mother at a garage sale.

Curiously, collectors do not and generally cannot use their sets to watch television today. Most receivers are not in working order, and the serious collector would not wish to replace original, worn-out parts with modern parts, even if such parts were obtainable. It is perhaps ironic that the best of television's past requires the best of television's present technology to be viewable.

4
Useful Addresses

Academy of Motion Picture Arts and Sciences
8949 Wilshire Boulevard
Beverly Hills, California 90211
(213) 278-8990

Academy of Television Arts and Sciences
4605 Lankershim Boulevard
Suite 800
North Hollywood, California 91602
(818) 506-7880

The Advertising Council
625 Third Avenue
New York, New York 10022
(212) 758-0400

Aladdin Books and Memorabilia
P.O. Box 152/122 W. Commonwealth Avenue
Fullerton, California 92632
(714) 738-6115

American Broadcasting Companies
1330 Avenue of the Americas
New York, New York 10019
(212) 887-7777
and
2040 Avenue of the Stars
Century City, California 90067
(213) 557-7777

American Federation of Television and Radio Artists
1350 Avenue of the Americas
New York, New York 10019
(212) 265-7700

American Film Institute
The John F. Kennedy Center for the Performing Arts
Washington, D.C. 20566
(202) 828-4044
and
P.O. Box 27999/2021 Northwestern Avenue
Los Angeles, California 90027
(213) 856-7600

Anglia Television
Anglia House
Norwich, NR1 3JG
England
NORWICH 615151

ATAS/UCLA Television Archives
Department of Theater Arts
University of California
Los Angeles, California 90024
(213) 206-8013

The Autograph Alcove
6907 W. North Avenue
Wauwatosa, Wisconsin 53213
(414) 771-7844
(Autograph dealer)

B & B Nostalgia
14621 East Poulter Drive
Whittier, California 90604
(213) 941-8309
(Autograph dealer)

Robert F. Batchelder
One West Butler Avenue
Ambler, Pennsylvania 19002
(215) 643-1430
(Autograph dealer)

Lynn Becker
P.O. Box 385
La Mirada, California 90637
(213) 943-9380
(Comic character memorabilia)

Bijou
10250 Santa Monica Boulevard
Century City, California 90067
(213) 277-0637
(Memorabilia dealer)

Blackhawk Films
Davenport, Iowa 52808
(319) 323-9736

Book Castle
200 N. Golden Mall
Burbank, California 91502
(818) 845-1563
(Book and memorabilia dealer)

Book City
6625 Hollywood Boulevard
Hollywood, California 90028
(213) 466-1049
(Book and memorabilia dealer)

The Book Sail
1186 N. Tustin Street
Orange, California 92667
(714) 997-9511
(Book dealer)

Border Television
The Television Centre
Carlisle, CAI 3NT
Cumbria
England
(0228) 25101

Eddie Brandt's Saturday Matinee
6310 Colfax Avenue
North Hollywood, California 91606
(818) 506-4242
(Photographs and old TV shows)

British Broadcasting Corporation
Television Centre
Wood Lane
London W12
England
(01) 743-8000
and
630 Fifth Avenue
New York, New York 10020
(212) 581-7100

Broadcast Pioneers
320 West 57th Street
New York, New York 10019
(212) 586-2000

Budget Films
4590 Santa Monica Boulevard
Los Angeles, California 90029
(213) 660-0187

CBS, Inc.
51 West Fifty-second Street
New York, New York 10019
(212) 975-4321
and
7800 Beverly Boulevard
Los Angeles, California 90036
(213) 852-2345

Children's Television Workshop
One Lincoln Plaza
New York, New York 10023
(212) 595-3456

Cinemabilia
611 Broadway
New York, New York 10012
(212) 533-6686
(Book and memorabilia dealer)

The Cinema Bookshop
13-14 Great Russell Street
London WCI
England
(01) 637-0206
(Book and memorabilia dealer)

Collectors Book Store
7014 Sunset Boulevard
Hollywood, California 90028
(213) 467-3296
(Photographs and memorabilia)

Corporation for Public Broadcasting
1111 Sixteenth Street, NW
Washington, D.C. 20036
(202) 293-6160

A.E. Cox
21 Cecil Road
Itchen
Southampton, SO2 7HX
England
(0703) 447989
(Book dealer)

Drama Books
511 Geary Street
San Francisco, California 94102
(415) 441-5343
(Book dealer)

Drama Bookshop
723 Seventh Avenue
New York, New York 10019
(212) 944-0595

Larry Edmunds Bookshop
6658 Hollywood Boulevard
Hollywood, California 90028
(213) 463-3273
(Book and memorabilia dealer)

Frederick M. Evans
3301 South Bear Street, #44E
Santa Ana, California 92704
(714) 979-9387
(Autograph dealer)

Federal Communications Commission
1919 M Street, NW
Washington, D.C. 20054
(202) 632-7000

John Fitton
One Orchard Way
Hensall, near Goole
North Humberside
England
("Dr. Who" memorabilia)

Fricelli Associates
P.O. Box 247
Bath Beach Station
Brooklyn, New York 11214
(212) 266-0675
(Autograph dealer)

Gotham Book Mart
41 West Forty-seventh Street
New York, New York 10036
(212) 719-4448

Granada Television Ltd.
36 Golden Square
London W1
England
(01) 734-8080

Hake's Americana & Collectibles
P.O. Box 1444
York, Pennsylvania 17405
(717) 848-1333
(Memorabilia auctions)

Beverly A. Hamer
P.O. Box 75
East Derry, New Hampshire 03041
(603) 432-3528
(Sheet music dealer)

Charles Hamilton
250 West Fifty-seventh Street
New York, New York 10019
(212) 245-7313
(Autograph dealer)

Hampton Books
Route 1, Box 76
Newberry, South Carolina 29108
(803) 276-6870
(Book dealer)

Douglas J. Hart
7278a Sunset Boulevard
Hollywood, California 90046
(213) 876-6070
(Photographs)

Paul Hartunian
65 Christopher Street
Montclair, New Jersey 07042
(201) 746-9132
(Autograph dealer)

David Henry
36 Meon Road
London W3 8AN
England
(Book dealer)

Hollywood Book and Poster Company
1706 North Las Palmas Avenue
Hollywood, California 90028
(213) 465-8764

Hollywood Poster Exchange
965 N. La Cienega Boulevard
Los Angeles, California 90069
(213) 657-2461

Independent Broadcasting Authority
70 Brompton Road
London SW3 1EY
England
(01) 584-7011

International Television Almanac
Quigley Publishing Company
159 West Fifty-third Street
New York, New York 10019
(212) 247-3100

Elliot M. Katt
8570½ Melrose Avenue
Los Angeles, California 90069
(213) 652-5178
(Book dealer)

Library of Congress
Motion Picture, Broadcasting, and Recorded Sound Division
Washington, D.C. 20540
(202) 287-5840

Limelight Bookstore
1803 Market Street
San Francisco, California 94103
(415) 864-2265

Lincoln Enterprises
P.O. Box 69470
Los Angeles, California 90069
("Star Trek" memorabilia)

Herbert Linder
55 Park Avenue
New York, New York 10016
(212) 685-2571
(Book dealer)

London Weekend Television
South Bank Television Centre
Kent House
Upper Ground
London SE1 9LT
England
(01) 261-3434

The Memory Shop
P.O. Box 364
New York, New York 10003
(212) 473-2404
(Photographs)

Memory Shop West
1755 Market Street
San Francisco, California 94103
(415) 626-4873
(Photographs and memorabilia)

Metromedia, Inc.
One Harmon Plaza
Secaucus, New Jersey 07094
(201) 348-3244

Miscellaneous Man
(George Theofiles)
Box 1776
New Freedom, Pennsylvania 17349
(717) 235-4766
(Poster and memorabilia dealer)

Motion Picture and Television Country House and Hospital
23450 Calabasas Road
Woodland Hills, California 91364
(818) 347-1591

Movie Star News
P.O. Box 191
New York, New York 10276
(212) 777-5564
(Photographs)

Museum of Broadcasting
One East Fifty-third Street
New York, New York 10022
(213) 752-4690

Museum of Modern Art
11 West Fifty-third Street
New York, New York 10019
(212) 708-9600

National Academy of Television Arts and Sciences
110 West Fifty-seventh Street
New York, New York 10019
(212) 586-8424

National Association of Broadcasters
1771 N Street, NW
Washington, D.C. 20036
(202) 293-3500

National Association of Television Program Executives, Inc.
310 Madison Avenue
Suite 1207
New York, New York 10017
(212) 661-0270

National Broadcasting Company, Inc.
30 Rockefeller Plaza
New York, New York 10020
(212) 664-4444

National Video Clearinghouse, Inc.
100 Lafayette Drive
Syosset, New York 11791
(516) 364-3686

NEWSREEL
c/o Bob Bennett
One Governor's Lane
Shelburne, Vermont 05482

Pacific Pioneer Broadcasters
6255 Sunset Boulevard
Suite 609
Hollywood, California 90028
(213) 461-2121

Kit Parker Films
1245 Tenth Street
Monterey, California 93940
(403) 649-5573

Lynn Pruett
Route 1, Box 51c
Beeville, Texas 78102
(512) 358-2581
(Autograph dealer)

Public Broadcasting Service
475 L'Enfant Plaza West
SW Washington, D.C. 20024
(202) 488-5000

R & R Enterprises
P.O. Box 52
Newton Centre, Massachusetts 02159
(617) 969-6040
(Autograph dealer)

Radio Telefis Eireann
Donnybrook
Dublin 4
Eire
(01) 693111

Jerry S. Redlich
3201 SW Fourth Street
Miami, Florida 33135
(305) 442-8538
(Autograph dealer)

Reel Images
456 Monroe Turnpike
Monroe, Connecticut 06468
(203) 261-5022
(Old television shows)

A & C Reuter
64 Spencer Road
Mitcham, Surrey
England
(01) 640-8630
(Autograph dealer)

Stephen Sally
P.O. Box 646
Times Square Station
New York, New York 10036
(212) 246-4976
(Photographs)

Scottish Television
Courcaddens
Glasgow
Scotland
GLASGOW 332-9999

Searle's Autographs
P.O. Box 630
St. Marys, Georgia 31558
(912) 882-5036

Society of Motion Picture and Television Engineers
862 Scarsdale Avenue
Scarsdale, New York 10583
(914) 472-6606

Richard Stoddard
90 East Tenth Street
New York, New York 10003
(212) 982-9440
(Book dealer)

Strand Book Store
828 Broadway
New York, New York 10003
(212) 473-1452

Sy Sussman
2962 South Mann Street
Las Vegas, Nevada 89102
(702) 873-2574
(Autograph dealer)

C. Sutherland
15 Aldridge Road Villas
London W11 1BL
England
(01) 221-0091
(Book dealer)

Television Index
150 Fifth Avenue
New York, New York 10011
(212) 924-0320

Television Information Office
745 Fifth Avenue
New York, New York 10022
(212) 759-6800

Thames Television
Thames Television House
306-318 Euston Road
London NW1 3BB
England
(01) 287-9494

TV Guide
Radnor, Pennsylvania 19088

UCLA Television Archives, *see* ATAS/UCLA Television
    Archives

Ulster Television, Ltd.
Havelock House
Ormeau Road
Belfast BT7 1EB
Northern Ireland
BELFAST 28122

Universal Autograph Collectors Club
P.O. Box 467
Rockville Centre, New York 11571

Video Dimensions
110 East Twenty-third Street
New York, New York 10010
(Old TV shows)

Peter Wood
20 Stonehill Road
Great Shelford
Cambridge, CB2 5JL
England
(0223) 842419
(Book dealer)

Yorkshire Television Ltd.
The Television Centre
Leeds, LS3 1JS
England
(0532) 438283

5
A Television Bibliography

No bookshops specialize exclusively in television. The best sources for television-related material are those establishments that deal primarily in film or theatre, such as Larry Edmunds Bookshop in Hollywood and Cinemabilia and Richard Stoddard in New York. Also worth checking out are two general bookshops, Book City in Hollywood and Strand in New York. To keep up to date on television books in print, readers are advised to subscribe to *Communication Booknotes,* edited by Christopher H. Sterling and published by the Center for Telecommunications Studies, George Washington University, Washington, D.C. 20052. *Communication Booknotes* tries to cover all titles in the field, as well as books about film, communications, popular culture, public relations, and journalism. A subscription is $20 for twelve issues.

In the following bibliography, books relating to television repairs, television equipment, communications, and mass media have been excluded, as have non-English-language volumes. Biographies and autobiographies have been included if the personality involved is clearly a television celebrity rather than a film celebrity who also happens to have done some television work. The average price of an out-of-print television-related book is $10. For books that are worth more than that, I have included a value based on prices quoted in dealers' catalogs. For books currently in print, the price quoted is that listed in *Books in Print.* Currently, television books decrease in value immediately after going out of print, but they may increase in value in years to come.

The 1946 American Television Directory, a fascinating volume including a useful history of television and a detailed bibliography. $30.

General

Ace, Goodman. *The Book of Little Knowledge.* New York: Simon and Schuster, 1955.

Adams, Charles. *Producing and Directing for Television.* New York: Henry Holt, 1953.

Adams, William, and Fay Schreibman, eds. *Television Network News.* Washington, D.C.: George Washington University, 1978. **$6.50.**

Allan, Doug. *How to Write for Television.* New York: E.P. Dutton, 1946. **$12.50.**

American Business Consultants, Inc. *Red Channels.* New York: Counterattack, 1950. **$25.**

Ames, Stanley William, and D.C. Birkinshaw. *Television Engineering, Principles and Practice.* London: Iliffe, 1953.

Anderson, Chuck. *The Electronic Journalist.* New York: Praeger, 1973.

——————. *Video Power.* New York: Praeger, 1975.

Anderson, Kent. *Television Fraud: The History and Implications of the Quiz Show Scandals.* Westport, Conn.: Greenwood Press, 1978. **$27.50.**

Andrews, Bart, and Brad Dunning. *The Worst TV Shows — Ever.* New York: E.P. Dutton, 1980.

Anner, George E. *Elements of Television Systems.* New York: Prentice-Hall, 1951.

Arlen, Michael J. *Living-Room War.* New York: Viking Press, 1969. Paperback edition, Penguin Books, 1982. **$5.95.**

——————. *The View from Highway I.* New York: Farrar, Straus and Giroux, 1976. **$8.95.**

——————. *The Camera Age: Essays on Television.* New York: Farrar, Straus and Giroux, 1981. **$13.95.** Paperback edition, Penguin Books, 1982. **$5.95.**

Arnold, Frank A. *Broadcast Advertising: The Fourth Dimension — Television Edition.* New York: John Wiley & Sons, 1933. **$15.**

Arons, Leon and Mark A. May, eds. *Television and Human Behavior.* New York: Appleton-Century-Crofts, 1963.

Averson, Richard, and David Manning White. *Electronic Drama.* Boston: Beacon Press, 1971.

Bailey, K.V. *The Listening Schools.* London: British Broadcasting Corporation, 1957.

Bailey, Robert Lee. *An Examination of Prime Time Network Television Special Programs, 1948 to 1966.* New York: Arno Press, 1980. **$15.**

Baker, Thomas Thorne. *Wireless Pictures and Television.* New York: Van Nostrand, 1927. **$25.**

Baldwin, Huntley. *Creating Effective TV Commercials.* Chicago: Crain Books, 1982. **$24.95.**

Baran, Stanley J. *The Viewer's Television Book.* Cleveland, Ohio: Penrith, 1980. **$6.95.**

Barnouw, Erik. *The Television Writer.* New York: Hill & Wang, 1962.

——————. *Tube of Plenty.* New York: Oxford University Press, 1975. **$22.50.** Paperback edition **$9.95.**

——————. *The Sponsor.* New York: Oxford University Press, 1978. **$17.95.** Paperback edition **$5.95.**

Bartlett, Sir Basil. *Writing for Television.* London: W.H. Allen, 1955.

Becker, Samuel L., and H. Clay Harshbarger. *Television.* New York: Henry Holt, 1958. **$15.**

Beitman, Morris N. *Most-Often Needed F.M. and Television Servicing Information.* Chicago: Supreme Publications, 1948. **$15.**

Bendick, Jeanne and Robert. *Television Works Like This.* New York: Whittlesey House, 1949. Revised editions published in 1954, 1959, and 1965.

Benson, Thomas William. *Fundamentals of Television.* New York: Mancall, 1930. **$20.**

Berger, Arthur Asa. *Television as an Instrument of Terror.* New Brunswick, N.J.: Transaction Books, 1980. **$6.95.**

Bettinger, Hoyland. *Television Techniques.* New York: Harper, 1947. Second edition, with Sol Cornberg, published in 1955.

Bluem, A. William. *Documentary in American Television: Form, Function, Method.* New York: Hastings House, 1965.

——————. *Religious Television Programs: A Study in Relevance.* New York: Hastings House, 1968. **$5.50.**

Bluem, A. William, and Roger Manvell, eds. *Television: The Creative Experience.* New York: Hastings House, 1967.

Blum, Richard A. *Television Writing.* New York: Hastings House, 1980. **$15.95.** Paperback edition **$8.95.**

Blumenthal, Norman. *The TV Game Shows.* New York: Pyramid, 1975.

Boetin, Michael, and David M. Rice, eds. *Network Television and the Public Interest.* Lexington, Mass.: Lexington Books, 1980.

Bolen, Murray Otto. *Fundamentals of Television.* Hollywood, Calif.: Hollywood Radio Publishers, 1950.

Book, Albert C., and Norman D. Cary. *The Television Commercial: Creativity and Craftsmanship.* New York: Decker, 1970.

——————. *The Radio and Television Commercial.* Chicago: Crain Books, 1978.

Borgman, Paul. *TV, Friend or Foe?* Elgin, Ill.: Cook, 1979. **$3.95.**

Bretz, Rudolf. *Techniques of Television Production.* New York: McGraw-Hill, 1953. Second Edition 1962. **$27.50.**

——————. *Handbook for Producing Educational and Public-Access Programs for Cable Television.* Englewood Cliffs, N.J.: Educational Technology Publications, 1976. **$19.95.**

Bretz, Rudolf, and Edward Stasheff. *Television Scripts for Staging and Study.* New York: Wyn, 1953.

Broaderick, Edwin B. *Your Place in TV.* New York: David McKay, 1954.

Brown, Les. *Television.* New York: Harcourt Brace, 1971. Paperback edition, 1973. **$4.95.**

_____. *Keeping Your Eye on Television.* New York: Pilgrim Press, 1979. **$4.95.**

Brown, Les, and Savannah Waring Walker, eds. *Fast Forward: The New Television Age and American Society.* New York: Andrews and McMeel, 1983. **$9.95.**

Buchsbaum, Walter H. *Fundamentals of Television.* New York: Rider, 1964. Second edition 1974.

Burrows, Thomas D., and Donald N. Wood. *Television Production: Disciplines and Techniques.* Dubuque, Iowa: W.C. Brown, 1978. Second edition 1982.

Busch, H. Ted, and Terry Landeck. *The Making of a Television Commercial.* New York: Macmillan, 1981. **$10.95.**

Caldwell-Clements, Inc. *Get Ready To Sell Television.* New York: Caldwell-Clements, 1944.

Cameron, James. *Radio and Television.* London: Cameron, 1932. **$25.**

_____. *Television for Beginners.* London: Cameron, 1940. **$20.** Revised edition 1947.

Camm, F. J. *Television and Short Wave Handbook.* Brooklyn, N.Y.: Brooklyn Chemical Publishing Company, 1942.

_____. *Television Manual.* Brooklyn, N.Y.: Chemical Publishing Company, 1943. **$15.**

Campbell, Robert. *The Golden Years of Broadcasting.* New York: Charles Scribner's Sons, 1976.

Cantor, Muriel G. *The Hollywood TV Producer: His Work and His Audience.* New York/London: Basic Books, 1971.

_____. *Prime-Time Television: Content and Control.* Beverly Hills, Calif.: Sage Publications, 1980. **$15.**

Carnegie Commission on Educational Television. *Public Television: A Program for Action.* New York: Harper and Row, 1967.

Cass, Ronald A. *Revolution in the Wasteland: Value and Diversity in Television.* Charlottesville, Va.: University Press of Virginia, 1981. **$10.**

Castleman, Harry, and Walter J. Podrazik. *Watching TV: Four Decades of American Television.* New York: McGraw-Hill, 1982. **$22.95.** Paperback edition **$14.95.**

_____. *Five Hundred Five Television Questions Your Friends Can't Answer.* New York: Walker, 1983. Paperback edition **$3.95.**

Cater, Douglass J., and Michael J. Nyhan, eds. *The Future of Public Broadcasting.* New York: Praeger, 1976. **$34.95.** Paperback edition **$13.95.**

Chappelle, Harry John Barton. *Television for the Amateur Constructor.* London: Sir Isaac Pitman and Sons, 1934. **$15.**

Cheney, Glenn A. *Television in American Society.* New York: Franklin Watts, 1983. **$8.90.**

Coakley, Mary Lewis. *Rated X: The Moral Case Against TV.* New Rochelle, N.Y.: Arlington House, 1977.

Cocking, W.T. *Television Receiving Equipment.* London: Iliffe, 1947. Revised edition 1950.

Coe, Michelle E. *How To Write for Television.* New York: Crown, 1980.

Cogley, John. *Report on Blacklisting: II, Radio — Television.* New York: The Fund for the Republic, 1956. **$15.**

Colby, Lewis. *The Television Director/Interpreter.* New York: Hastings House, 1968.

Cole, Barry G., comp. *Television.* New York: Free Press, 1970.

_____. *Television Today: A Closeup View; Readings from TV Guide.* New York: Oxford University Press, 1981. **$22.50.** Paperback edition **$9.95.**

Coleman, Howard W., ed. *Color Television.* New York: Hastings House, 1968.

Collins, A. Frederick. *Experimental Television.* Boston: Lothrop, 1932. **$15.**

Combes, Peter, and John Tiffin. *Television Production for Education.* London: Focal Press, 1978. **$27.95.**

Comstock, George. *Television in America.* Beverly Hills, Calif.: Sage Publications, 1980. **$15.** Paperback edition **$7.95.**

_____. *Television and Human Behavior.* New York: Columbia University Press, 1978. **$12.50.**

Conrad, John J. *The Television Commercial: How It Is Made.* New York: Van Nostrand Reinhold, 1983.

Conrad, Peter, ed. *Television: The Medium and Its Manners.* Boston: Routledge and Kegan Paul, 1982. **$12.95.**

Cooke, David Coxe. *Behind the Scenes in Television.* New York: Dodd, Mead, 1958.

Coombs, Charles Ira. *Window on the World.* Cleveland, Ohio: World, 1965.

Coppa, Frank J., ed. *Screen and Society: The Impact of Television upon Aspects of Contemporary Civilization.* Chicago: Nelson-Hall, 1980. **$20.95.**

Corbett, Scott. *What Makes TV Work?* Boston: Little, Brown, 1965.

Costello, Lawrence F., and George N. Gordon. *Teach with Television.* New York: Hastings House, 1961.

Cousin, Michelle. *Writing a Television Play.* Boston: The Writer, 1975. **$12.**

Cowan, Geoffrey. *See No Evil.* New York: Simon and Schuster, 1979. Paperback edition, Touchstone, 1980. **$4.95.**

Crawley, Chetwode. *From Telegraphy to Television.* London: Frederick Warne, 1931. **$20.**

Cross, Donna Woolfolk. *Mediaspeak.* New York: Coward-McCann, 1983. **$13.95.**

Cross, Ellis Royal. *Underwater Photography and Television.* New York: Exposition Press, 1954.

Cruger, Paul. *Key to Television Writing.* Hollywood, Calif.: The Author, 1940.

_____. *Television "How" for the Writer-Producer.* 1945.

David, Eugene. *Television and How It Works.* Englewood Cliffs, N.J.: Prentice-Hall, 1962.

Davis, Desmond. *The Grammar of Television Production.* London: Barrie, 1960. Revised edition 1974.

De Forest, Lee. *Television, Today and Tomorrow.* New York: The Dial Press, 1942. **$20.**

De Franco, Ellen B. *TV On/Off.* Santa Monica, Calif.: Goodyear, 1980. **$8.95.**

Denman, Frank. *Television, The Magic Window.* New York: Macmillan, 1952.

Deutscher, J. Noel. *Your Future in Television*. New York: Richards Rosen Press, 1963.

Dinsdale, Alfred. *First Principles of Television*. New York: John Wiley and Sons, 1932. **$25.**

——————. *Television*. London: Sir Isaac Pitman and Sons, 1926. **$30.**

Dizard, Wilson P. *Television, A World View*. Syracuse, N.Y.: Syracuse University Press, 1966.

Dome, Robert B. *Television Principles*. New York: McGraw-Hill, 1951.

Donner, Stanley T., ed. *The Meaning of Commercial Television*. Austin, Tex.: University of Texas, 1967.

Draper, Benjamin. *Television*. San Francisco: California Academy of Sciences, 1953.

Duerr, E. *Radio and Television Acting*. New York: Rinehart, 1950. **$37.50.**

Dunbar, Janet. *Script-Writing for Television*. London: Museum Press, 1965.

Dunlap, Orrin E., Jr. *The Outlook for Television*. New York: Harper and Bros., 1932. **$30.**

——————. *The Future of Television*. New York: Harper and Bros., 1942. **$15.** Revised edition 1947.

——————. *Understanding Television*. New York: Greenberg, 1948.

Dupuy, Judy. *Television Show Business*. Schenectady, N.Y.: General Electric, 1945. **$20.**

Eckhardt, George. *Electronic Television*. Chicago: Goodheart-Wilcox, 1936. **$15.**

Eddy, Captain William C. *Television: The Eyes of Tomorrow*. New York: Prentice-Hall, 1945. **$15.**

Edgar, David. *Ah! Mischief*. London: Faber and Faber, 1982. *The Eighth Art*. New York: Henry Holt, 1962.

Eliot, Marc. *American Television*. Garden City, N.Y.: Anchor Press, 1981. **$15.95.**

——————. *Televisions: One Season in American Television*. New York: St. Martin's Press, 1983. **$12.95.**

Elliott, Philip. *The Making of a Television Series*. New York: Hastings House, 1973. **$25.** Paperback edition **$12.50.**

Elliott, William Y., ed. *Television's Impact on American Culture*. East Lansing, Mich.: Michigan State University Press, 1956.

Ellis, John. *Visible Functions: Cinema, Television and Video*. Boston: Routledge and Kegan Paul, 1983. **$10.50.**

Ellison, Harlan. *The Glass Teat*. New York: Ace Books, 1970. Second Edition, Pyramid, 1975.

Emery, Walter Byron. *Broadcasting and Government*. East Lansing, Mich.: Michigan State University Press, 1961. Revised edition 1971. Paperback edition **$8.50.**

——————. *National & International Systems of Broadcasting: Their History, Operaton & Control*. East Lansing, Mich.: Michigan State University Press, 1969. Paperback edition **$8.75.**

Emmens, Carol A. *An Album of Television*. New York: Franklin Watts, 1980.

Englander, A. Arthur, and Paul Petzold. *Filming for Television*. New York: Hastings House, 1976. **$21.50.**

Ewing, Sam, in collaboration with R.W. (Ozzie) Abolin. *Don't Look at the Camera!* Blue Ridge Summit, Pa.: TAB Books, 1973.

Felix, Edgar H. *Television: Its Methods and Uses*. New York: McGraw-Hill, 1930. **$15.**

Fields, Alice. *Television*. New York: Franklin Watts, 1980. **$8.60.**

Fink, Donald G. *Principles of Television Engineering*. New York: McGraw-Hill, 1940.

——————. *Television Standards and Practise*. New York: McGraw-Hill, 1943.

——————. *Television Engineering*. New York: McGraw-Hill, 1952. **$45.**

Fink, Donald G., and David M. Lutyens. *The Physics of Television*. Garden City, N.Y.: Anchor Books, 1960.

Fireman, Judy, ed. *TV Book*. New York: Workman, 1977. Paperback edition **$7.95.**

Fishman, Ed. *How To Strike It Rich on TV Game Shows*. Los Angeles: Price, Stern, Sloan, 1972.

Fiske, John, and John Hartley. *Reading Television*. London: Methuen, 1978. Paperback edition **$6.95.**

Fowler, Kenneth. *Television Fundamentals*. New York: McGraw-Hill, 1953.

Fowles, Jib. *Television Viewers vs. Media Snobs*. New York: Stein and Day, 1982. **$16.95.**

Franks, A. H. *Ballet for Film and Television*. London: Sir Isaac Pitman & Sons, 1950.

Freeman, Don. *In a Flea's Navel*. San Diego, Calif.: A.S. Barnes, 1980. **$8.95.**

Gable, Luther S.H. *The Miracle of Television*. Chicago: Wilcox, 1949. **$15.**

Galanoy, Terry. *Down the Tube*. Chicago: Henry Regnery, 1970.

Gardner, Richard M. *Be on TV*. New York: Day, 1960.

Gattegno, Caleb. *Towards a Visual Culture; Educating Through Television*. New York: Discus/Avon, 1969. Revised edition 1971. **$6.95.** Paperback edition **$1.65.**

Gilbert, Robert E. *Television and Presidential Policies*. North Quincy, Mass.: Christopher Publishing House, 1972.

Gilmore, Art, and Glenn Y. Middleton. *Television and Radio Announcing*. Hollywood, Calif.: Hollywood Radio Publishers, 1949. **$12.50.**

Gitlin, Todd. *Vertical Hold: Inside Prime-Time TV*. New York: Pantheon Books, 1983. **$16.95.**

Glasford, Glen H. *Fundamentals of Television Engineering*. New York: McGraw-Hill, 1955.

Glick, Ira O., and Sidney J. Levy. *Living with Television*. Chicago: Aldine, 1962.

Glut, Donald F., and Jim Harmon. *The Great Television Heroes*. Garden City, N.Y.: Doubleday, 1975.

Goethals, Gregor T. *The TV Ritual*. Boston: Beacon Press, 1981. **$12.02.** Paperback edition **$6.97.**

Goldsmith, Alfred Norton. *Television Status and Trends*. New York: Association of National Advertisers, 1949.

Goldstein, Stan and Fred, eds. *The TV Guide Quiz Book*. New York: Bantam Books, 1978.

Gorham, Maurice. *Television, Medium of the Future.* London: Marshall, 1949. **$22.50.**

Gould, Jack. *All About Radio and Television.* New York: Random House, 1953. Second edition 1958.

Green, Timothy. *The Universal Eye.* New York: Stein and Day, 1972. **$12.50.**

Greene, Robert S. *Television Writing: Theory and Practice.* New York: Harper and Bros., 1952. Second edition 1956.

Greenfield, Jeff. *Television: The First Fifty Years.* New York: Harry Abrams, 1977.

Grob, Bernard. *Basic Television.* New York: McGraw-Hill, 1949. Second edition 1954. Third edition 1964. Fourth edition 1975. Fifth edition 1984. **$28.95.**

Gross, Ben. *I Looked and I Listened.* New York: Random House, 1954.

Halloran, Arthur Hobart. *Television with Cathode-Rays.* San Francisco: Pacific Radio Publishing Company, 1936. **$15.**

Hansen, Gerald L. *Introduction to Solid-State Television Systems.* Englewood Cliffs, N.J.: Prentice-Hall, 1969.

Harding, C.F. *The Purdue University Experimental Television System.* Lafayette, Ind.: Purdue University, 1939.

Harvey, Tad. *Television: How It Works.* New York: Putnam, 1968.

Hathaway, K.A. *Television: A Practical Treatise.* Chicago: American Technical Society, 1933. **$15.**

Hawker, John Patrick. *Radio and Television.* New York: Hart, 1966.

Hawks, Ellison. *The Book of Electrical Wonders.* New York: The Dial Press, 1935. **$17.50.**

Hazard, Patrick D., ed. *TV as Art.* Champaign, Ill.: National Council of Teachers of English, 1966.

Heath, Eric. *Writing for Television.* Los Angeles: Research Publishing Company, 1950. Second edition 1953.

——————. *Television Writer's Handbook.* Los Angeles: Brewster, 1963.

Heighton, Elizabeth W., and Don R. Cunningham. *Advertising in the Broadcast and Cable Media.* Belmont, Calif.: Wadsworth Publishing, 1984. **$21.95.**

Helt, Scott. *Practical Television Engineering.* New York: Murray Hill Books, 1950. Second edition 1953.

Herzog, David Alan. *Collecting Today for Tomorrow.* New York: Arco, 1980.

Higgins, A.P. *Talking about Television.* London: British Film Institute, 1966. Distributed in the U.S. by New York Zoetrope. **$6.**

Hilliard, Robert L. *Writing for Television and Radio.* Belmont, Calif.: Wadsworth Publishing, 1984. **$18.95.**

Himmelstein, Harold. *On the Small Screen.* New York: Praeger, 1981. **$27.95.**

Hodapp, William C. *The Television Actor's Manual.* New York: Appleton-Century-Crofts, 1955. **$12.50.**

Hoggart, Richard, and Janet Morgan, eds. *The Future of Broadcasting.* New York: Holmes & Meier, 1982. **$29.50.**

Horner, Rosalie. *Inside BBC Television.* London: British Broadcasting Corporation/Exeter, Devon: Webb & Bower, 1983. **$25.**

Hubbell, Richard F. *4000 Years of Television.* New York: G.P. Putnam's Sons, 1942. **$30.**

——————. *Televison Programming and Production.* New York: Murray Hill Books, 1945. **$20.** Second edition 1950. **$15.**

Hurell, Ron. *Van Nostrand Reinhold Manual of Television Graphics.* New York: Van Nostrand Reinhold, 1973.

Hutchinson, Robert W. *Easy Lessons in Television.* London: W.B. Clive/University Tutorial Press, 1930. **$15.**

——————. *Television Up-to-Date.* London: University Tutorial Press, 1937. **$15.**

Hutchinson, Thomas H. *Here Is Television, Your Window to the World.* New York: Hastings House, 1946. Second edition 1950.

Hyde, Stuart. *Television and Radio Announcing.* Boston: Houghton Mifflin, 1984. **$24.95.**

Hylander, C.J., and Robert Harding. *An Introduction to Television.* New York: Macmillan, 1941. **$15.**

Iezzi, Frank. *Understanding Television Production.* Englewood Cliff, N.J.: Prentice-Hall, 1984. **$18.95.** Paperback edition **$9.95.**

Jackson, K.G., ed. *Newnes Book of Video.* London/Boston: Newnes, 1980.

James, Clive. *Visions Before Midnight.* London: Jonathan Cape, 1977.

——————. *The Crystal Bucket.* London: Jonathan Cape, 1981.

James, W.C. *Television in Transition.* Chicago: Crain Books, 1982. **$74.95.**

Jaspersohn, William. *A Day in the Life of a Television News Reporter.* Boston: Little, Brown, 1981. **$9.95.**

Jenkins, Charles Francis. *Radiomovies, Radiovision, Television.* Washington, D.C.: National Capital Press, 1929. **$25.**

Jones, Eufron C. *Television Magic.* New York: Viking Press, 1978. **$11.50.**

Jones, Peter. *The Technique of the Television Cameraman.* New York: Hastings House, 1965. Third edition 1972. **$29.95.**

Kahn, Frank J., ed. *Documents of American Broadcasting.* Englewood Cliffs, N.J.: Prentice-Hall, 1984. **$24.95.**

Katzman, Henry M., and William Hansen, eds. *BMI Television Sketchbook.* New York: Broadcast Music, 1951. **$15.**

Kaufman, William Irving. *How To Write for Television.* New York: Hastings House, 1955.

Kellock, H. *Television.* Washington, D.C.: Editorial Research Reports, 1944.

Kelly, Katie. *My Prime Time.* New York: Seaview Books, 1980.

Kennedy, Philip D. *Understanding Television.* Indianapolis: Sams, 1976. Paperback editon **$4.95.**

Kerby, Philip. *The Victory of Television.* New York: Harper & Bros., 1939. **$15.**

Kerkhof, Frederick. *Television.* New York: Elsevier House, 1952.

Kingston, Walter K., and Rome Cowgill. *Television Acting and Directing.* New York: Henry Holt, 1965.

Kiver, Milton. S. *Television Simplified*. New York: Van Nostrand, 1946. Second edition 1948. Third edition 1950. Fourth edition 1954. Fifth edition 1955. Sixth edition 1962. Seventh edition 1973.

Krasnow, Erwin G., and Lawrence D. Longley. *The Politics of Broadcast Regulation*. New York: St. Martin's Press, 1973. Third edition 1982. **$17.95.** Paperback edition **$9.95.**

Lackmann, Ron. *Remember Television*. New York: G.P. Putnam, 1971.

Landau, Rosejane. *The TV Machine*. Los Angeles: Masters, 1973.

Lane, Henry Milton. *The Boston Post Book on Television*. Boston: Boston Post, 1928. **$20.**

Larner, E. T. *Practical Television*. New York: Van Nostrand, 1928. **$25.**

Laughton, Roy. *TV Graphics*. London: Studio Vista/New York: Reinhold, 1966.

Lawrence, J. *Off Mike*. New York: Essential Books, 1944.

Lee, Robert E. *Television: The Revolution*. New York: Essential Books, 1944. **$15.**

Legg, Stuart, and Robert Fairthorne. *Cinema and Television*. London: Longmans Green, 1939. **$20.**

Lerch, John H., ed. *Careers in Broadcasting*. New York: Appleton-Century-Crofts, 1962.

Lesher, Stephen. *Media Unbound: The Impact of Television Journalism on the Public*. Boston: Houghton Mifflin, 1982. **$13.95.**

Levin, Richard. *Television by Design*. London: Bodley Head, 1961.

Levinson, Richard, and William Link. *Stay Tuned*. New York: St. Martin's Press, 1981. **$11.95.** Paperback edition **$2.95.**

Lewis, Gregg A. *Telegarbage*. Nashville, Tenn.: Nelson, 1977.

Lichty, Lawrence W., and Malachi C. Topping. *American Broadcasting*. New York: Hastings House, 1975.

Liebert, Robert M., John N. Neale, and Emily S. Davidson. *The Early Window*. New York: Pergamon Press, 1973. Second edition 1982. **$25.** Paperback edition **$9.95.**

Lohr, Lenox Riley. *Television Broadcasting*. New York: McGraw-Hill, 1940.

Lowe, Carl, ed. *Television and American Culture*. New York: H. W. Wilson, 1981. **$10.**

Maloff, I.G., and D.W. Epstein. *Electron Optics in Television*. New York: McGraw-Hill, 1938.

Mander, Jerry. *Four Arguments for the Elimination of Television*. New York: William Morrow, 1978. Paperback edition **$5.95.**

Manvell, Roger. *On the Air: A Study of Broadcasting in Sound and Television*. London: Andre Deutsch, 1953.

Martin, Albert Victor Jean. *Technical Television*. Englewood Cliffs, N. J.: Prentice-Hall, 1962.

Matusow, Barbara. *The Evening Stars: The Making of the Network News Anchor*. Boston: Houghton Mifflin, 1983. **$14.95.**

Mayer, Martin. *About Television*. New York: Harper and Row, 1972.

McArthur, Colin. *Television & History*. London: British Film Institute, 1978. Distributed in the U.S. by New York Zoetrope. Paperback edition **$6.50.**

McMahan, Harry Wayne. *Television Production*. New York: Hastings House, 1957.

McNeil, Alex. *Total Television*. New York: Penguin Books, 1980.

McNulty, Edward N. *Television: A Guide for Christians*. Nashville, Tenn.: Abingdon Press, 1976.

—————. *When Television Is a Member of the Family*. New York: Abbey, 1981. **$2.45.**

Meagher, John R. *Television, Trouble-Shooting and Assignment*. Camden, N. J.: RCA, 1948.

Metz, Robert. *CBS: Reflections in a Bloodshot Eye*. Chicago: Playboy Press, 1975. **$17.50.**

Meyers, Richard. *The TV Detectives*. San Diego, Calif.: A.S. Barnes, 1981. **$25.** Paperback edition **$14.95.**

Milgram, Stanley, and R. Lance Shotland. *Television and Anti-Social Behavior*. New York: Academic Press, 1973. **$31.**

Miller, Merle. *The Judges and the Judged*. Garden City, New York: Doubleday, 1952. **$15.**

Miller, Merle, and Evan Rhodes. *Only You, Dick Darling!* New York: William Sloane Associates, 1964.

Millerson, Gerald. *The Technique of Television Production*. New York: Hastings House, 1961. **$15.**

—————. *TV Camera Operation*. New York: Hastings House, 1973.

—————. *Basic TV Staging*. New York: Hastings House, 1974. Second edition 1982. Paperback edition **$11.95.**

—————. *TV Lighting Methods*. New York: Hastings House, 1975. Second edition 1982. Paperback edition **$11.95.**

—————. *Effective TV Production*. New York: Hastings House, 1976. Second edition 1983. **$11.95.**

—————. *The Technique of Lighting for Television and Motion Pictures*. London/Boston: Focal Press, 1982. **$39.95.** Paperback edition **$21.95.**

Mitchell, Curtis. *Cavalcade of Broadcasting*. Chicago: Follett, 1970.

Montgomery, Robert. *Open Letter from a Television Viewer*. New York: James H. Heineman, 1968.

Morgenstern, Steve, ed. *Inside the TV Business*. New York: Sterling, 1979.

Morrison, David E., and Howard Tumbler. *Television & the Falklands*. London: British Film Institute, 1983. Distributed in the U.S. by New York Zoetrope. Paperback edition **$11.95.**

Moseley, Sydney A., and H.J.B. Chappelle. *Television Today and Tomorrow*. London: Sir Isaac Pitman & Sons, 1940. **$20.**

Moseley, Sydney A., and H. McKay. *Television: A Guide for the Amateur*. London: Oxford University Press, 1936. **$15.**

Moyers, James A., and John F. Wostrel. *Practical Radio, Including Television*. New York: McGraw-Hill, 1931. **$15.**

_____. *The Radio Handbook, Including Television and Sound Motion Pictures*. New York: McGraw-Hill, 1931. **$15.**

Muller, Robert, ed. *The Television Dramatist*. London: Elek, 1973.

Myers, L. M. *Television Optics*. London: Sir Isaac Pitman & Sons, 1936. **$15.**

NBC. *Television Talk*. New York: NBC, 1946. **$15.**

_____. *Television Today*. New York: NBC, 1951-1952. **$15.**

Nash, Bruce M. *Thirty Years of Television*. New York: Drake, 1976.

_____. *Tubeteasers*. South Brunswick, N.J.: A.S. Barnes, 1979.

Nash, Constance, and Virginia Oakey. *The Television Writer's Handbook*. New York: Harper and Row, 1978. **$11.95.** Paperback edition **$4.95.**

Newcomb, Horace. *TV: The Most Popular Art*. Garden City, N.Y.: Anchor Press, 1974. Paperback edition **$4.95.**

_____. *Television: The Critical View*. New York: Oxford University Press, 1982. **$9.95.**

The 1946 American Television Directory. New York: American Television Society, 1946. **$30.**

Noll, Edward M. *Television for Radiomen*. New York: Macmillan, 1949. Revised edition 1955.

Noll, Roger G., Merton J. Peck, and John J. McGowan. *Economic Aspects of Television Regulation*. Washington, D.C.: Brookings Institute, 1973.

Norris, Roy C. *Television To-Day*. London: Rockliff, 1947. **$15.**

Ogden, Warde B. *The Television Business*. New York: Ronald, 1961.

Paletz, Donald A., Roberta E. Pearson, and Donald L. Willis. *Politics in Public Service Advertising on Television*. New York: Praeger, 1977.

Paulu, Burton. *British Broadcasting: Radio & Television in the United Kingdom*. Minneapolis, Minn.: University of Minnesota Press, 1956. **$15.**

_____. *Radio & Television Broadcasting in Eastern Europe*. Minneapolis, Minn.: University of Minnesota Press, 1974. **$25.**

_____. *Television & Radio in the United Kingdom*. Minneapolis, Minn.: University of Minnesota Press, 1981. **$39.50.**

Porterfield, John, and Kay Reynolds, eds. *We Present Television*. New York: Norton, 1940. **$20.**

Pennell, Ellen La Verne. *Women on TV*. Minneapolis, Minn.: Burgess, 1954.

Powers, Ron. *The Newscasters: The News Business as Show Business*. New York: St. Martin's Press, 1978. Paperback edition **$4.95.**

_____. *Supertube: The Rise of Television Sports*. New York: Coward McCann, 1984. **$17.95.**

Price, Jonathan. *The Best Thing on TV, Commercials*. New York: Viking Press, 1978. **$17.95.**

Primeau, Ronald. *The Rhetoric of Television*. New York: Longman, 1978. Paperback edition **$12.95.**

Quinlan, Sterling. *Inside ABC: American Broadcasting Company's Rise to Power*. New York: Hastings House, 1979. **$12.95.**

RCA Institute, Inc. *Television*. New York: RCA Institute's Technical Press, 1936. **$15.**

Rabinoff, Carter V., and Magdalena E. Wolbrecht. *Questions and Answers in Television Engineering*. New York: McGraw-Hill, 1950.

Ranney, Austin. *Channels of Power: The Impact of Television on American Politics*. New York: Basic Books, 1983. **$14.95.**

Rather, Dan, and Mickey Kerskowitz. *The Camera Never Blinks*. New York: Morrow, 1977. **$15.**

Ravage, John W. *Television: The Director's Viewpoint*. Boulder, Colorado: Westview Press, 1978. **$12.50.**

Reel, A. Franks. *The Networks: How They Stole the Show*. New York: Charles Scribner's Sons, 1979.

Richards, Vyvyan. *From Crystal to Television, "The Electron Bridge."* London: A. & C. Black, 1928.

Roberts, Edward Barry. *Television Writing and Selling*. Boston: The Writer, 1954. Second edition 1957. Fourth edition 1964. Fifth edition 1967.

Ross, Rodger J. *Color Films for Color Television*. New York: Hastings House, 1970. **$13.95.**

Ross, Wallace A. *Best TV Commercials of the Year*. New York: The American TV Commercials Festival, 1967.

Rotha, Paul, ed. *Television in the Making*. New York: Hastings House, 1956.

Rovin, Jeff. *The Signet Book of TV Lists*. New York: Signet, 1982. Paperback edition **$1.95.**

_____. *TV Babylon*. New York: Signet, 1984. **$5.95.**

Ruiter, Jacob H. *What You Should Know about Television*. Somerville, N.J.: Ruiter, 1952.

Rutstein, Nat. *Go Watch TV!* New York: Sheed, 1974.

Sass, Lauren, ed. *Television: The American Medium in Crisis*. New York: Facts on File, 1979. **$19.95.**

Schafer, Kermit. *Kermit Schafer's Blunderful World of Bloopers*. New York: Bounty Books, 1973.

_____. *Kermit Schafer's All Time Great Bloopers*. New York: Avenel Books, 1973.

_____. *Kermit Schafer Presents Blooper Tube*. New York: Crown, 1979.

Scheraga, Morton G., and Joseph J. Roche. *Video Handbook*. Montclair, N.J.: Boyce, 1949.

Schure, Alexander. *Basic Television*. New York: Rider, 1958.

Seldes, Gilbert. *The Great Audience*. New York: Viking Press, 1950.

_____. *Writing for Television*. Garden City, N.Y.: Doubleday, 1952.

Settel, Irving. *Best Television Humor of the Year*. New York: Wyn, 1956.

_____, ed. *How To Write Television Comedy*. Boston: The Writer, 1958.

Shales, Tom. *On the Air!* New York: Summit Books, 1982. **$14.95.**

Shanks, Bob. *The Coolfire: How To Make It in Television*. New York: W.W. Norton, 1976. Paperback edition **$4.95.**

Shayon, Robert Lewis. *Television and Our Children*. New York: Longmans, 1951.

—————. *Open to Criticism*. Boston: Beacon Press, 1971.

—————. *The Crowd-Catchers*. New York: Saturday Review Press, 1973.

Sheldon, H. Horton, and Edgar Norman Grisewood. *Television*. New York: Van Nostrand, 1929. **$20.**

Sherrington, Richard. *Television and Language Skills*. London: Oxford University Press, 1978.

Shulman, Arthur, and Roger Youman. *How Sweet It Was*. New York: Shorecrest, 1966.

Simon, Ernest. *The B.B.C. from Within*. London: Victor Gollancz, 1953.

Singer, Dorothy G., Jerome Singer, and Diana M. Zuckerman. *Teaching Television*. New York: The Dial Press, 1981. **$10.95.**

Sklar, Robert. *Prime-Time America*. New York: Oxford University Press, 1980. **$19.95.** Paperback edition **$5.95.**

Skornia, Harry J. *Television and Society*. New York: McGraw-Hill, 1965.

Skornia, Harry J., and Jack W. Kitson, eds. *Problems and Controversies in Television and Radio*. Palo Alto, Calif.: Pacific Books, 1974. Paperback edition **$3.95.**

Sleeper, Milton Blake. *The Television Handbook, Look and Listen*. New York: Henley, 1939. **$15.**

Slurzberg, Morris, and William Osterheld. *Essentials of Electricity for Radio and Television*. New York: McGraw-Hill, 1950.

Smith, Anthony, ed. *British Broadcasting*. Newton Abbot, Devon: David & Charles, 1974.

Solotaire, Robert Spencer. *How To Get into Television*. New York: Sheridan House, 1957.

Southwell, John. *Getting a Job in Television*. New York: McGraw-Hill, 1947. **$12.**

Sposa, Louis A. *Television Primer of Production and Direction*. New York: McGraw-Hill, 1947.

Stavins, R., ed. *Television Today: The End of Communication and the Death of Community*. Mt. Rainier, Maryland: Gryphon House, 1971. **$10.**

Stein, Benjamin. *The View from Sunset Boulevard*. New York: Basic Books, 1979. Paperback edition **$4.50.**

Steiner, Gary. *The People Look at Television*. New York: Alfred A. Knopf, 1963. **$17.50.**

Stevens, Paul. *I Can Sell You Anything*. New York: Wyden, 1972.

Stoddard, Edward. *The First Book of Television*. New York: Watts, 1955. Revised edition, under title of *Television*, 1970. Summer Television Advertising. New York: NBC, 1952.

Sutton, Shawn. *The Largest Theatre in the World*. London: British Broadcasting Corporation, 1982.

Swinson, Arthur. *Writing for Television Today*. London: A. & C. Black, 1963.

Taylor, John Russell. *Anatomy of a Television Play*. London: Weidenfeld and Nicholson, 1962. **$42.50.**

Teague, Bob. *Live and Off-Color*. New York: A & W, 1982. **$14.95.**

Television Newsgathering. New York: Society of Motion Picture and Television Engineers, 1976.

Television USA: 13 Seasons. New York: Museum of Modern Art, 1962.

Thomas, Howard. *With an Independent Air*. London: Weidenfeld and Nicholson, 1977.

Thomas, Lowell. *Magic Dials*. New York: Lee Furman, 1939. **$15.**

Trapnell, Coles. *Teleplay: An Introduction to Television Writing*. San Francisco: Chandler, 1966. Revised edition, Hawthorn Books, 1974. Paperback edition **$7.95.**

Tyers, Paul D. *Television Reception Technique*. London: Sir Isaac Pitman & Sons, 1937.

Tyler, Kingdom S. *Telecasting and Color*. New York: Harcourt, 1946.

Tyler, Poyntz, ed. *Television and Radio*. New York: H.W. Wilson, 1961.

Udelson, Joseph H. *The Great Television Race*. Alabama: University of Alabama Press, 1982. **$18.95.**

Ullyett, Kenneth. *Radio & TV*. London: Baker, 1971.

Uslan, Michael, and Bruce Solomon. *The TV Trivia Quiz Book*. New York: Harmony Books, 1979.

WBKB, Chicago's Pioneer TV Station. Chicago: WBKB, 1941. **$15.**

Wade, Robert J. *Designing for TV*. New York: Pellegrini & Cudahy, 1952. **$17.50.**

—————. *Staging TV Programs and Commercials*. New York: Hastings House, 1954.

Wainwright, Charles Anthony. *Television Commercials*. New York: Hastings House, 1970.

Waldrop, Frank C., and Joseph Borkin. *Television: A Struggle for Power*. New York: William Morrow, 1938. **$15.**

Weinberg, Meyer. *TV in America*. New York: Ballantine Books, 1962.

Weiss, Ann E. *Tune In, Tune Out*. Boston: Houghton Mifflin, 1981. **$8.95.**

Weiss, Margaret R. *The TV Writer's Guide*. New York: Pellegrini & Cudahy, 1952.

Westin, Av. *Newswatch: How TV Decides the News*. New York: Simon and Schuster, 1982. **$6.95.**

Whelan, Kenneth. *How the Golden Age of Television Turned My Hair to Silver*. New York: Walker, 1973.

White, David Manning, and Richard Averson, eds. *Sight, Sound and Society*. Boston: Beacon Press, 1968.

White, Gordon. *Video Techniques*. London/Boston: Newnes, 1982. **$31.95.**

White, Hooper. *How To Produce an Effective TV Commercial*. Chicago: Crain Books, 1981. **$25.95.**

White, Melvin R. *Beginning Television Production*. Minneapolis, Minn.: Burgess, 1953.

Wilcox, Desmond. *Ten Who Dared*. Boston: Little Brown, 1977. **$15.**

Wilk, Max. *The Golden Age of Television.* New York: Delacorte Press, 1976. **$15.**

Wilkins, Joan A. *The TV Guide-Away.* Pearl River, N.Y.: Roan Press, 1975. Paperback edition **$3.95.**

——————. *Breaking the TV Habit.* New York: Charles Scribner's Sons, 1982. **$9.95.** Paperback edition **$4.95.**

Williams, Martin T. *TV, The Casual Art.* New York: Oxford University Press, 1982. **$17.95.**

Williams, Raymond. *Television: Technology and Cultural Form.* New York: Schocken Books, 1974. **$7.50.** Paperback edition **$4.95.**

Willis, Edgar E. *Foundatons in Broadcasting: Radio and Television.* New York: Oxford University Press, 1951.

Wilson, John Charles. *Television Engineering.* London: Sir Isaac Pitman & Sons, 1937.

Witek, John W. *Response Television.* Chicago: Crain Books, 1981. **$22.95.**

Wurtzel, Alan. *Television Production.* New York: McGraw-Hill, 1979. Second edition 1983. **$26.95.**

Wylie, Max. *Writing for Television.* New York: Cowles, 1970.

Yates, Raymond Francis. *A.B.C. of Television.* New York: Norman W. Henley, 1929. **$20.**

——————. *New Television, The Magic Screen.* New York: Didier, 1948. **$15.**

Yurko, J.T. *Video Basics.* Englewood Cliffs, N.J.: Prentice-Hall, 1983. **$8.95.**

Zettl, Herbert. *Television Production Handbook.* Belmont, Calif.: Wadsworth Publishing, 1984. **$26.95.**

Zworykin, V.K., and G.A. Morton. *Television.* New York: John Wiley, 1940. **$20.** Second edition 1954. **$15.**

Reference

Allan, Angela and Elkan. *The Sunday Times Guide to Movies on Television*. London: Book Club Associates, 1980.

BBC. *British Broadcasting: A Bibliography*. London: British Broadcasting Corporation, 1958.

Baden, Anne L. *Television: A Selected List of Recent Writings*. Washington, D.C.: Library of Congress, 1938.

Barnouw, Erik. *A Tower in Babel*. New York: Oxford University Press, 1966. **$22.50.**

——————. *The Golden Web*. New York: Oxford University Press, 1968. **$22.50.**

——————. *The Image Empire*. New York: Oxford University Press, 1970. **$22.50.**

Barrett, Elizabeth P. *Radio and Television Bibliography*. New York: ANTA, 1953.

Battison, John P. *Movies for TV*. New York: Macmillan, 1950. **$12.50.**

Beitman, Morris N. *Television Cyclopedia*. Chicago: Supreme Publications, 1939. **$25.**

Blum, Daniel. *Pictorial History of Television*. Philadelphia: Chilton Company, 1959. **$25.**

Brandt, George W., ed. *British Television Drama*. New York: Cambridge University Press, 1981. **$49.50.** Paperback edition **$15.95.**

Brooks, Tim, and Earle Marsh. *The Complete Directory to Prime Time Network TV Shows, 1946-Present*. New York: Ballantine Books, 1979. **$19.95.** Paperback edition, 1981, **$12.95.**

Brown, Les. *Les Brown's Encyclopedia of Television*. New York: Zoetrope, 1983. **$29.95.** Paperback edition **$16.95.**

CBS Reference Library. *Radio and Television Bibliography*. New York: CBS, 1941. (First published in 1937 as *Radio Broadcasting Bibliography*.)

Castlemam, Harry, and Walter J. Podrazik. *The TV Schedule Book*. New York: McGraw-Hill, 1984. **$24.95.** Paperback edition **$14.95.**

Coyne Electrical School. *Coyne Technical Dictionary of 4000 Terms Used in Television, Radio, Electricity, Electronics*. Chicago: Coyne, 1955. **$15.**

Crist, Judith. *Judith Crist's TV Guide to the Movies*. New York: Popular Library, 1974.

David, Nina, comp. *TV Season: 74-75*. Phoenix, Ariz.: Oryx Press, 1976. **$25.**

——————. *TV Season: 75-76*. Phoenix, Ariz.: Oryx Press, 1977. **$11.95.**

——————. *TV Season: 76-77*. Phoenix, Ariz.: Oryx Press, 1978. **$11.95.**

——————. *TV Season: 77-78*. Phoenix, Ariz.: Oryx Press, 1979. **$11.95.**

Diamant, Lincoln. *Television's Classic Commercials; The Golden Years, 1948-1958*. New York: Hastings House, 1971.

——————. *The Broadcast Communications Dictionary*. New York: Hastings House, 1978 (second edition). **$10.95.**

Dispenza, Joseph. *Reruns*. New York: Benziger, 1970.

Drucker, Malka, and Elizabeth James. *Series TV*. New York: Clarion Books, 1983. **$11.95.**

Dunlap, Orrin E. *Radio & Television Almanac*. New York: Harper and Bros., 1951. **$25.**

Eisner, Joel, and David Krinsky. *Television Comedy Series*. Jefferson, N.C.: McFarland, 1984. **$49.95.**

Essoe, Gabe. *The Book of TV Lists*. Westport, Conn.: Arlington House, 1981. Paperback edition **$8.95.**

Fielding, Raymond, comp. *A Technological History of Motion Pictures and Television*. Berkeley: University of California Press, 1967. **$40.**

Friedman, Favius. *Great Movies on TV*. New York: Scholastic Book Services, 1972.

Gianakos, Larry James. *Television Drama Series Programming: A Comprehensive Chronicle, 1959-1975*. Metuchen, N.J.: Scarecrow Press, 1978. **$35.**

——————. *Television Drama Series Programming: A Comprehensive Chronicle, 1947-1959*. Metuchen, N.J.: Scarecrow Press, 1980. **$32.**

——————. *Television Drama Series Programming: A Comprehensive Chronicle, 1975-1980*. Metuchen, N.J.: Scarecrow Press, 1981. **$25.**

——————. *Television Drama Series Programming: A Comprehensive Chronicle, 1980-1982*. Metuchen, N.J.: Scarecrow Press, 1983. **$45.**

Godfrey, Donald G. *A Directory of Broadcast Archives*. Washington, D.C.: Broadcast Education Association, 1983. **$5.**

Goldstein, Fred and Stan. *Prime-Time Television: A Pictorial History from Milton Berle to "Falcon Crest."* New York: Crown, 1983. **$25.**

Halliwell, Leslie. *Halliwell's Teleguide*. London/New York: Granada, 1979.

Harris, Jay S. *TV Guide: The First 25 Years*. New York: Simon and Schuster, 1978. Paperback edition, Plume, 1980, **$9.95.**

I.T.V. *Guide to Independent Television*. London: I.T.V., 1973.

International TV & Video Guide. London: Tantivy Press/New York: New York Zoetrope, 1983 to present. **$9.95.**

International Television Almanac. New York: Quigley Publications, 1956 to present. Current edition **$47.** Back issues **$15-25.**

Kempner, Stanley, ed. *Television Encyclopedia*. New York: Fairchild, 1948. **$20.**

Kemp's International Film and Television Year Book. London: Kemp's, 1973-1974 to present. Current edition **$50.** Back issues **$15-25.**

Kent, George. *Motion Picture and Television Directory.* Hollywood: American Society of Cinematographers, 1980.

Leonard, William T. *Theatre: Stage to Screen to Television.* Metuchen, N.J.: Scarecrow Press, 1981. **$74.50.**

Levitan, Eli L. *An Alphabetical Guide to Motion Picture, Television, and Videotape Production.* New York: McGraw-Hill, 1970.

Lewis, E. J. G. *Television: Technical Terms and Definitions.* London: Sir Isaac Pitman & Sons, 1936. **$20.**

MacDonald, J. Fred. *Blacks and White TV: Afro-Americans in Television since 1948.* Chicago: Nelson-Hall, 1983. **$23.95.** Paperback edition **$11.95.**

McLanachan, William, ed. *Television and Radar Encyclopedia.* New York: Pitman, 1954.

Maltin, Leonard. *TV Movies.* New York: New American Library, 1984. Paperback edition **$4.95.** Earlier editions 1969, 1974, 1978, 1980, 1982 (have no value).

Marill, Alvin H. *Movies Made for Television.* New York: New York Zoetrope, 1984. **$29.95.**

McCavitt, William. *Radio and Television: A Selected Annotated Bibliography — Supplement One, 1977-1981.* Metuchen, N.J.: Scarecrow Press, 1982. **$12.**

Meehan, Diana M. *Ladies of the Evening: Women Characters of Prime-Time Television.* Metuchen, N.J.: Scarecrow Press, 1983. **$16.**

Michael, Paul, and James Robert Parish. *The Emmy Awards: A Pictorial History.* New York: Crown, 1970. **$15.**

National Radio Institute. *Radio-Television-Electronics Dictionary.* New York: Rider, 1962.

National Video Clearinghouse, Inc. *The Video Source Book.* Syosset, N.Y.: National Video Clearinghouse, 1983 (fifth edition). **$125.** Paperback edition **$28.**

Neidhart, Peter. *Technical Dictionary of Television Engineering, Television Electronics.* New York: Macmillan, 1964.

Noble, Peter, ed. *The British Film & Television Year Book,* 1955-56 to present. London: Gordon White, 1955-56 — 1956-57. London: British and American Film, 1957-58 — 1973-74. London: Cinema TV Today, 1975-76. London: King Publications: 1975-76 — 1977-78. London: Screen International, 1978-79 to present (first published as *British Film Yearbook*).

Norback, Craig T. and Peter G. *TV Guide Almanac.* New York: Ballantine Books, 1980.

Parish, James Robert. *Actors Television Credits 1950-1972.* Metuchen, N.J.: Scarecrow Press, 1973. **$27.50.**

Parish, James Robert, and Mark Trost. *Actors' Television Credits Supplement I.* Metuchen, N.J.: Scarecrow Press, 1978. **$21.**

Parish, James Robert, and Vincent Terrace. *Actors' Television Credits: Supplement II, 1977-1981.* Metuchen, N.J.: Scarecrow Press, 1982. **$22.50.**

Perry, Jeb H. *Universal Television: The Studio and Its Programs, 1950-1980.* Metuchen, N.J.: Scarecrow Press, 1983. **$32.50.**

Post, Joyce A. *TV Guide 25 Year Index, April 3, 1953-December 31, 1977.* Radnor, Pa.: Triangle Publications, 1979.

Poteen, G. Howard. *Published Radio, Television, and Film Scripts: A Bibliography.* Troy, N.Y.: Whitston, 1975.

Rose, Ernest D. *World Film & Television Resources.* Bonn: Friedrich-Ebert-Stiftung, 1974.

Rose, Oscar. *Radio Broadcasting and Television: An Annotated Bibliography.* New York: H.W. Wilson, 1947.

Rovin, Jeff. *The Great Television Series.* South Brunswick, N.J.: A.S. Barnes, 1977.

Scheuer, Steven H. *TV: The Television Annual, 1978-79.* New York: Macmillan, 1979.

———————. *Who's Who in Television and Cable.* New York: Facts on File, 1983. **$49.95.**

———————. *Movies on TV.* New York: Bantam Books, 1984. Paperback edition **$7.98.** Earlier editions 1958, 1961, 1966, 1968, 1971, 1974, 1977, 1981 (have no value).

Settel, Irving, ed. *Top TV Shows of the Year, 1954-1955.* New York: Hastings House, 1955. **$15.**

———————. *A Pictorial History of Television.* New York: Frederick Ungar, 1983. **$24.95.** First edition 1969.

Sharp, Harold S. and Marjorie Z. Sharp. *Index to Characters in the Performing Arts. Part IV — Radio and Television.* Metuchen, N.J.: Scarecrow Press, 1973. **$22.50.**

Smith, Myron J., Jr. *U.S. Television Network News: A Guide to Sources in English.* Jefferson, North Carolina: McFarland, 1984. **$29.95.**

Spottiswoode, Raymond, ed. *The Focal Encyclopedia of Film & Television Techniques.* New York: Hastings House, 1969. **$64.95.**

Steinberg, Cobbett. *TV Facts.* New York: Facts on File, 1980. **$19.95.**

TV Guide Roundup. New York: Holt, Rinehart and Winston, 1960.

Terrace, Vincent. *The Complete Encyclopedia of Television Programs 1947-1979.* South Brunswick, N.J.: A.S. Barnes, 1979. **$29.95.**

———————. *Television 1970-1980.* San Diego, Calif.: A.S. Barnes, 1981. **$22.50.**

Thompson, Howard, ed. *The New York Times Guide to Movies on TV.* Chicago: Quadrangle Books, 1970. **$15.**

U.N.E.S.C.O. *Television, a World Survey.* Paris: U.N.E.S.C.O., 1953.

University of Southern California. *Radio and Television Holdings of the University Library.* Los Angeles: University of Southern California, 1961.

Who's Who on Television. London: Independent Television Books, 1980. Second edition 1982.

Soap Operas

Angel, Velma. *Those Sensational Soaps.* Brea, Calif.: Uplift Books, 1983. **$4.95.**

Cantor, Muriel G., and Suzanne Pingree. *The Soap Opera.* Beverly Hills, Calif.: Sage Publications, 1983. **$29.95.** Paperback edition **$9.95.**

Cassata, Mary B., and Thomas Skill. *Life on Daytime Television.* New York: Ablex, 1983. **$27.50.** Paperback edition **$14.95.**

Denis, Paul, ed. *Daytime TV's Star Directory.* New York: Popular Library, 1976.

Edmondson, Madeleine, and David Rounds. *The Soaps: Daytime Serials of Radio and Television.* New York: Stein and Day, 1973. Second edition 1976.

Gilbert, Annie. *All My Afternoons.* New York: A & W, 1979. **$14.95.** Paperback edition **$7.95.**

Groves, Seli. *Soaps.* Chicago: Contemporary Books, 1983. Paperback edition **$9.95.**

Kutler, Jane, and Patricia Kearney. *Super Soaps.* New York: Grosset and Dunlap, 1977.

LaGuardia, Robert. *The Wonderful World of TV Soap Operas.* New York: Ballantine Books, 1974.

——————. *From Ma Perkins to Mary Hartman: The Illustrated History of Soap Operas.* New York: Ballantine Books, 1977.

——————. *Soap World.* New York: Arbor House, 1983. **$22.95.**

Meyers, Richard, *Super TV Stars.* New York: Drake, 1977.

——————. *The Illustrated Soap Opera Companion.* New York: Drake, 1977.

The Official Soap Opera Annual. New York: Ballantine Books, 1977 to present.

Soares, Manuela. *The Soap Opera Book.* New York: Harmony Books, 1978.

Wakefield, Dan. *All Her Children.* New York: Doubleday, 1976.

Biography/Autobiography

This section is limited to celebrities closely associated with television. Those personalities whose careers have embraced television secondary to motion pictures have not been included.

Allen, Steve. *Mark It and Strike It*. New York: Henry Holt, 1960.

Berle, Milton, and Haskel Frankel. *Milton Berle: An Autobiography*. New York: Delacorte, 1974. Paperback edition, Dell, 1975.

Bishop, James. *The Golden Ham: A Candid Biography of Jackie Gleason*. New York: Simon and Schuster, 1956.

Blumenthal, John. *Anthony Geary*. New York: Wallaby Books, 1982. **$6.95.**

Bondercroft, John. *Barbara Walters: Today's Woman*. New York: Leisure Books, 1975. Paperback edition.

Caesar, Sid, and Bill Davidson. *Where Have I Been?* New York: Crown, 1982. **$12.95.**

Carpozi, George, Jr. *Vince Edwards*. New York: Belmont Books, 1962.

Clark, Dick, and Bill Libby. *Looking Great, Staying Young*. Indianapolis: Bobbs-Merrill, 1980.

Coakley, Mary Lewis. *Mister Music Maker, Lawrence Welk*. Garden City, N.Y.: Doubleday, 1958.

Cosell, Howard. *Like It Is*. Chicago: Playboy Press, 1974.

Donahue, Phil. *Donahue*. New York: Simon and Schuster, 1979. Paperback edition, Fawcett, 1981, **$2.95.**

Downs, Hugh. *Yours Truly*. New York: Holt, Rinehart and Winston, 1960.

Dreher, Carl. *Sarnoff: An American Success*. New York: Quadrangle/New York Times, 1977. (Biography of David Sarnoff).

Druxman, Michael B. *Merv*. New York: Award Books, 1976. Paperback edition **$1.95.**

Everson, George. *The Story of Television, the Life of Philo T. Farnsworth*. New York: W.W. Norton, 1949. **$15.**

Francis, Arlene, and Florence Rome. *A Memoir*. New York: Simon and Schuster, 1978.

Franklin, Joe. *A Gift for People*. New York: M. Evans, 1978. **$8.95.**

Friendly, Fred W. *Due to Circumstances Beyond Our Control. . .* New York: Random House, 1967.

Frischauer, Willi. *Will You Welcome Now. . .David Frost*. New York: Hawthorn Books, 1971.

Godfrey, Jean and Kathy. *Genius in the Family*. New York: Putnam, 1962. (Biography of Arthur Godfrey.)

Govoni, Albert. *The Lawrence Welk Story*. New York: Pocket Books, 1966. Paperback edition.

Green, Jonathon. *The Fonz & Henry Winkler*. New York: Bunch Books, 1978.

Griffin, Merv. *Merv*. New York: Simon and Schuster, 1980. Paperback edition **$2.95.**

Griffin, Merv, and Peter Barsocchini. *From Where I Sit*. New York: Arbor House, 1982. **$14.95.** Paperback edition **$3.50.**

Harris, Michael David. *Always on Sundays*. New York: Meredith Press, 1968. (Biography of Ed Sullivan.)

Houston, David. *Lindsay Wagner: Superstar of The Bionic Woman*. New York: Belmont Tower Books, 1976.

Johnson, George. *The Real Jack Paar*. New York: Gold Medal Books, 1962.

Katz, Susan. *The Lawrence Welk Scrapbook*. New York: Grosset and Dunlap, 1978.

_____. *TV's Superwoman Scrapbook*. New York: Tempo, 1978. Paperback edition **$1.25.**

_____. *Kristy and Jimmy: TV's Talented McNichols*. New York: Grosset and Dunlap, 1979.

_____. *The Erik Estrada Scrapbook*. New York: Tempo, 1980. Paperback edition **$1.95.**

Kendrick, Alexander. *Prime Time: The Life of Edward R. Murrow*. Boston: Little, Brown, 1969.

King, Norman. *Dan Rather*. New York: Leisure Books, 1981. **$2.25.**

Kurtis, Bill. *On Assignment*. Chicago: Rand McNally, 1983. **$19.95.**

Lardine, Robert. *He-e-e-er's Johnny*. New York: Award Books, 1975. (Biography of Johnny Carson.)

Lewis, Barbara and Dan. *Barbara Walters: TV's Superlady*. New York: Pinnacle Books, 1976. Paperback edition.

Linkletter, Art, and Dean Jennings. *Confessions of a Happy Man*. New York: Bernard Geis, 1960.

Lorence, Douglas. *Johnny Carson*. New York: Drake, 1975.

Lyons, Eugene. *David Sarnoff*. New York: Harper & Row, 1966.

Marx, Arthur. *Red Skelton*. New York: E.P. Dutton, 1979.

McKay, Jim. *My Wide World*. New York: Macmillan, 1973.

McMahon, Ed, and Carroll Carroll. *Here's Ed*. New York: Putnam, 1976.

Morella, Joe, and Edward Z. Epstein. *Lucy*. Secaucus, N.J.: Lyle Stuart, 1973 (Biography of Lucille Ball.)

Munshower, Suzanne. *Hollywood's Newest Superstar — Henry Winkler*. New York: Berkeley Medallion, 1976.

Nelson, Ozzie. *Ozzie*. Englewood Cliffs, N.J.: Prentice-Hall, 1973.

Oakes, Philip. *Tony Hancock*. London: The Woburn Press, 1975.

Paar, A. H. *The Lennon Sisters*. Garden City, N.Y.: Doubleday, 1960.

Paar, Jack. *I Kid You Not*. Boston: Little, Brown, 1960. Paperback edition, Pocket Books, 1961.

_____. *My Saber Is Bent*. New York: Trident Press, 1961.

_____. *P.S. Jack Paar*. Garden City, N.Y.: Doubleday, 1983. **$14.95.**

Paley, William. *As It Happened: A Memoir*. Garden City, N.Y.: Doubleday, 1979.

Pruetzel, Maria, and John A. Barbour. *The Freddie Prinze Story*. Kalamazoo, Mich.: Master's Press, 1978.

Reasoner, Harry. *Before the Colors Fade.* New York: Alfred A. Knopf, 1981. **$11.50.** Paperback edition **$5.95.**

Reyburn, Wallace. *Frost: Anatomy of a Success.* London: Macdonald, 1968. (Biography of David Frost.)

Robinson, Richard. *New TV Super Stars.* New York: Pyramid Books, 1974.

Rollin, Betty. *Am I Getting Paid for This?* Boston: Little, Brown, 1982. **$14.95.**

Sarnoff, David. *Looking Ahead.* New York: McGraw-Hill, 1968.

Savitch, Jessica. *Anchorwoman.* New York: G.P. Putnam's Son, 1982. **$12.95.** Paperback edition **$2.95.**

Schwienher, William K. *Lawrence Welk — An American Institution.* Chicago: Nelson-Hall, 1980.

Silvers, Phil, and Robert Saffron. *This Laugh Is on Me.* Englewood Cliffs, N.J.: Prentice-Hall, 1973.

T., Mr. *Mr. T.* New York: St. Martin's Press, 1984. **$12.95.**

Tennis, Craig. *Johnny Tonight!* New York: Pocket Books, 1980. Paperback edition. (Biography of Johnny Carson.)

Wallace, Mike, and Gary Paul Gates. *Close Encounters.* New York: William Morrow, 1984. **$17.95.**

Walley, David G. *The Ernie Kovacs Phile.* New York: Bolder, 1979. First published in 1975 by Drake as *Nothing in Moderation.*

Welk, Lawrence. *Guidelines for Successful Living.* Minneapolis, Minn.: Denison, 1968.

Welk, Lawrence, and Bernice McGeehan. *Wunnerful, Wunnerful!* Englewood Cliffs, N.J.: Prentice-Hall, 1971.

——————. *Ah-One, Ah-Two!* Englewood Cliffs, N.J.: Prentice-Hall, 1974.

——————. *My America, Your America.* Englewood Cliffs, N.J.: Prentice-Hall, 1976.

——————. *Lawrence Welk's Musical Family Album.* Englewood Cliffs, N.J.: Prentice-Hall, 1977.

——————. *This I Believe.* Englewood Cliffs, N.J.: Prentice-Hall, 1979. Paperback edition **$2.75.**

——————. *You're Never Too Young.* Englewood Cliffs, N.J.: Prentice-Hall, 1981. **$9.95.**

Whicker, Alan. *Within Whicker's World.* London: Elm Tree Books, 1982. **$22.50.**

Wilmut, Roger. *Tony Hancock 'Artiste.'* London: Eyre Methuen, 1978.

Wilson, Earl. *The NBC Book of Stars.* New York: Pocket Books, 1957.

Winkler, Henry. *The Other Side of Henry Winkler.* New York: Warner Books, 1976.

Wolf, Warner, and William Taaffe. *Gimme a Break!* New York: McGraw-Hill, 1983. **$14.95.**

Zehnpfennig, Gladys. *Lawrence Welk, Champagne Music Man.* Minneapolis, Minn.: Denison, 1968.

Individual Shows and Series

Note: There is a separate listing for "Star Trek" in view of the amount of material on this series.

Alda, Alan. *The Last Days of Mash.* Verona, N.J.: Unicorn, 1983. Paperback edition **$9.95.**

Allen, Robert J., ed. *Four Contemporary Religious Plays.* Glen Rock, N.J.: Paulist Press, 1964.

Allen, Steve. *Meeting of Minds.* Los Angeles: Hubris House, 1978.

Andrews, Bart. *Lucy & Ricky & Fred & Ethel.* New York: E.P. Dutton, 1976.

——————. *The I Love Lucy Quizbook.* San Diego, Calif.: A.S. Barnes, 1981. Paperback edition **$5.95.**

Andrews, Bart, and Thomas J. Watson. *Loving Lucy.* New York: St. Martin's Press, 1980. **$15.** Paperback edition **$9.95.**

Applebaum, Irwyn. *The World According to Beaver.* New York: Bantam Books, 1984.

The Best Television Plays. New York: Merlin Press, 1949-1954. **$15.**

Bowles, Jerry. *A Thousand Sundays: The Story of the Ed Sullivan Show.* New York: G.P. Putnam's Sons, 1980.

Chayefsky, Paddy. *Television Plays.* New York: Simon and Schuster, 1955.

Cooke, Alistaire. *Masterpieces: A Decade of Masterpiece Theatre.* New York: Alfred A. Knopf, 1981. **$25.**

Costigan, James. *Two Plays.* New York: Simon and Schuster, 1959. **$22.50.**

Dicks, Terrance, and Malcolm Hulke. *The Making of Doctor Who.* London: W.H. Allen, 1980.

Ellis, Robin. *Making Poldark.* Bodmin, Cornwall: Bossiney Books, 1978.

Fates, Gil. *What's My Line.* Englewood Cliffs, N.J.: Prentice-Hall, 1978. Paperback edition **$3.95.**

Galanoy, Terry. *Tonight!* Garden City, N.Y.: Doubleday, 1972. ("The Tonight Show.")

Galton, Ray, and Alan Simpson. *Hancock's Half Hour.* London: Woburn Press, 1974.

Granada Television Ltd. *Granada's Manchester Plays.* Manchester: Manchester University Press, 1962.

Haining, Peter. *Twenty Years of Doctor Who.* London: W.H. Allen, 1983.

Hall, Willis. *The Television Playwright: Ten Plays for B.B.C. Television.* London: Michael Joseph, 1960.

Harris, Mark. *The Doctor Who Technical Manual.* New York: Random House, 1983. Paperback editions **$3.95** and **$5.99.**

Hoopes, Ned E., and Patricia Neale Gordon. *Great Television Plays.* New York: Dell, 1969 (Volume I) and 1975 (Volume II).

Jacobs, Will, and Garard Jones. *The Beaver Papers.* New York: Crown, 1983. Paperback edition **$4.95.**

Kalter, Suzy. *The Complete Book of M*A*S*H.* New York: Harry N. Abrams, 1984. **$27.50.**

Kelly, Richard. *The Andy Griffith Show.* Winston-Salem, N.C.: John F. Blair, 1981. Paperback edition **$7.95.**

Kneale, Nigel. *The Quatermass Experiment.* Harmondsworth, Middlesex: Penguin Books, 1959.

——————. *Quatermass and the Pit.* London: Arrow Books, 1960.

——————. *Quatermass II.* Harmondsworth, Middlesex: Penguin Books, 1960.

Leeman, Dickie. *What's My Line?* London: Allan Wingate, 1955. **$15.**

Lockwood, Daniel. *The Mary Hartman Story.* New York: Bolder, 1976. Paperback edition.

Madsen, Axel. *60 Minutes.* New York: Dodd, Mead, 1984. **$16.95.**

The Making of James Clavell's Shogun. New York: Delta, 1980. Paperback edition **$8.95.**

The Making of the Jewel in the Crown. New York: St. Martin's Press, 1983. **$14.95.**

Mandel, L. *Do Not Gentle into That Good Night.* Hollywood: CBS, 1967. **$27.50.**

Marland, Michael, ed. *Z Cars.* London: Longmans, 1968.

Metz, Robert. *The Today Show.* Chicago: Playboy Press, 1977.

Murrow, Edward R., and Fred W. Friendly, eds. *See It Now.* New York: Simon and Schuster, 1955.

Neyland, James. *The Official Battlestar Galactica Scrapbook.* New York: Grosset and Dunlap, 1978.

Owen, Alun. *Three TV Plays.* New York: Hill & Wang, 1963.

Perry, George. *Life of Python.* Boston: Little, Brown, 1983. **$9.95.**

The Prize Plays of Television, 1956. New York: Random House, 1956. **$12.50.**

Profiles in Courage. New York: Bantam Books, 1965.

Reiss, David S. *M*A*S*H: The Exclusive, Inside Story of T.V.'s Most Popular Show.* New York: Bobbs-Merrill, 1980. Paperback edition **$8.95.**

Road, Alan. *Doctor Who — The Making of a Television Series.* London: Andre Deutsch, 1982.

Rooney, Andrew A. *A Few Minutes with Andy Rooney.* New York: Atheneum, 1981. **$12.95.**

——————. *And More by Andy Rooney.* New York: Atheneum, 1982. **$12.95.**

Rose, Reginald. *Six Television Plays.* New York: Simon and Schuster, 1956.

Sanford, Herb. *Ladies and Gentlemen, the Gary Moore Show.* New York: Stein and Day, 1976.

Seabrook, Steven. *The Official Mork & Mindy Scrapbook.* New York: Wallaby, 1979.

Sennett, Ted. *Your Show of Shows.* New York: Macmillan, 1977.

Serling, Rod. *Patterns.* New York: Simon and Schuster, 1957.

Shakespeare, William, adapted by Michael Benthall and Ralph Nelson. *Hamlet: A Television Script.* New York: CBS, 1959. **$20.**

Skaggs, Calvin, ed. *The American Short Story.* New York: Dell, 1977 (Volume I) and 1980 (Volume II).

Trewin, J. C., ed. *Six Wives of Henry VIII.* New York: Frederick Ungar, 1972.

Tulloch, John, and Manuel Alvarado. *Doctor Who: The Unfolding Text.* New York: St. Martin's Press, 1984. **$9.95.**

Vidal, Gore, ed. *Best Television Plays.* New York: Ballantine Books, 1956. **$35.**

———. *Visit to a Small Planet, and Other Television Plays.* Boston: Little, Brown, 1956. **$30.**

Weissman, Ginny, and Coyne Steven Sanders. *The Dick Van Dyke Show.* New York: St. Martin's Press, 1983. **$22.50.**

Willis, Ted. *Woman in a Dressing Gown, and Other Television Plays.* London: Barrie, 1959.

Zicree, Marc Scott. *The Twilight Zone Companion.* New York: Bantam Books, 1982. **$9.95.**

Children and Television

Barcus, Francis Earle, and Rachel Wolkin. *Children's Television.* New York: Praeger, 1977.

Barcus, Francis Earle. *Images of Life on Children's Television.* New York: Praeger, 1983. **$21.95.**

Belson, William A. *Television Violence and the Adolescent Boy.* Farnborough, Hampshire: Saxon House, 1978. **$22.95.**

Berry, Gordon L., and Claudia Mitchell-Kernan, eds. *Television and the Socializaton of the Minority Child.* New York: Academic Press, 1982. **$25.**

Brown, Ray, ed. *Children and Television.* Beverly Hills: Sage Publications, 1976.

Cater, Douglass, and Stephen Strickland. *TV Violence and the Child.* New York: Russell Sage Foundation, 1975. **$7.95.**

Fischer, Stuart. *Kid's TV: The First 25 Years.* New York: Facts on File, 1983. **$19.95.**

Garry, Ralph. F.B. Rainsberry, and Charles Winick, eds. *For the Young Viewer.* New York: McGraw-Hill, 1962.

Howe, Michael I. *Television & Children.* Hamden, Conn.: Shoe String Press, 1977. **$12.**

Jacobsen, Karen. *Television.* Chicago: Children's Press, 1982.

Kaye, Evelyn. *The Family Guide to Children's Television.* New York: Pantheon Books, 1974.

——————. *The ACT Guide to Children's Television.* Boston: Beacon Press, 1979. Paperback edition **$5.95.**

Kelley, Michael R. *A Parent's Guide to Television: Making the Most of It.* New York: John Wiley, 1983. **$8.95.**

Melody, William H. *Children's Television.* New Haven: Yale University Press, 1973.

Moody, Kate. *Growing Up on Television.* New York: Times Books, 1980. **$12.95.**

Morris, Norman S. *Television's Child.* Boston: Little, Brown, 1971.

Schramm, Wilbur, Jack Lyle, and Edwin B. Parker. *Television in the Lives of Our Chidlren.* Stanford, Calif.: Stanford University Press, 1961.

Shayon, Robert Lewis. *Television and Our Children.* New York: Longmans, 1951.

Winick, Charles. *Children's Television Commercials.* New York: Praeger, 1973.

Winick, Mariann P. and Charles Winick. *The Television Experience: What Children See.* Beverly Hills, Calif.: Sage Publications, 1979. **$24.**

Woolery, George W. *Children's Television: The First Thirty-Five Years, 1946-1981.* Metuchen, N.J.: Scarecrow Press, 1983. **$27.50.**

"Star Trek"

Andrews, Bart. *Trekkie Quiz Book.* New York: New American Library, no date. Paperback edition **$1.95.**

Asherman, Allan. *The Star Trek Compendium.* New York: Wallaby Books, 1981.

Bailey, Margaret. *Live Long and Prosper: The Star Trek Phenomenon.* New Brunswick, N.J.: Rutgers University Graduate School of Library Science, 1976.

Blish, James. *The Star Trek Reader.* New York: E.P. Dutton, 1976.

Cahill, Vincent. *Meaning in Star Trek.* Chambersburg, Pa.: Anima Books, 1977.

Foster, Alan Dean. *Star Trek Log One.* Leyden, Mass.: Aeonian Press, 1974.

Gerrold, David. *The World of Star Trek.* New York: Bluejay Books, 1984. **$8.95.**

Goldstein, Stanley and Fred. *Star Trek Spaceflight Chronology.* New York: Pocket Books, 1980. Paperback edition.

Lichtenberg, Jacqueline, Sondra Marshek, and Joan Winston. *Star Trek Lives!* New York: Bantam Books, 1975.

Nimoy, Leonard. *I Am Not Spock.* Milbrae, Calif.: Celestial Arts, 1975.

The Official Price Guide to Star Trek and Star Wars Collectibles. Orlando, Fla.: House of Collectibles, 1983.

Razzi, James. *Star Trek Puzzle Manual.* Toronto: Bantam Books, 1976.

Sackett, Susan, ed. *Letters to Star Trek.* New York: Ballantine Books, 1977.

The Star Trek Guide. Mattituk, N.Y.: Aeonian Press, 1978.

Trexindex: An Index to Star Trek Fanzines. Brooklyn, N.Y.: Poison Pen Press, 1977.

Trimble, Bjo. *Star Trek Concordance of People, Places and Things.* Los Angeles: Mathom House, 1969.

Turnbull, Gerry, ed. *A Star Trek Catalog.* New York: Grosset and Dunlap, 1979.

Whitfield, Stephen E., and Gene Roddenberry. *The Making of Star Trek.* New York: Ballantine Books, 1968.

Winston, Joan. *The Making of the Star Trek Conventions.* Garden City, N.Y.: Doubleday, 1977.

Index

Italicized numbers refer to photographs or other illustrations.

About the Author

Anthony Slide has been called "a publishing phenomenon." Since 1971 he has written or edited more than twenty-five books on the history of the motion picture, vaudeville, radio, and the theatre, and, additionally, he edits the "Filmmakers" series of books published by the Scarecrow Press. He was co-founder and editor of *The Silent Picture*, the only serious quarterly devoted to the art and history of the silent film, and for five years contributed a monthly column to *Films in Review*. His articles have appeared in *American Cinematographer, American Film, Cineaste, Focus on Film, Gallery,* and the *Los Angeles Times*. He has contributed articles on such television personalities as Milton Berle, Lawrence Welk, and Betty White to *Emmy,* the journal of the Academy of Television Arts and Sciences.

Aside from his work as a writer, Anthony Slide has found time to serve as associate archivist of the American Film Institute, responsible for the acquisition and preservation of more than 2,000 films in the National Film Collection. He set up the 1911-1920 volume of the *American Film Institute Catalog,* and serves on the Catalog's advisory board. From 1975-1980, Slide was resident film historian of the Academy of Motion Picture Arts and Sciences, heading its National Film Information Service, coordinating major exhibits on subjects such as Costume Design and the 75th anniversary of Hollywood, and producing more than fifty special screenings devoted to such topics as the Will Rogers Centenary, Mary Pickford, Best Dance Direction, the W.C. Fields Centenary, Pete Smith, and Groucho Marx.

As a film programmer, he began his career with retrospectives devoted to British Cinema in the Twenties and British Music Hall Comedians on Film at London's National Film Theatre; in 1970 he organized Britain's first silent film festival, an eighteen-day event at the National Film Theatre, presented concurrently with the London Film Festival. He has presented film programs and lectured at the Museum of Modern Art, Columbia University, Pacific Film Archive, Filmex, and the Sinking Creek Film Celebration in Nashville, Tennessee.

As a filmmaker, Anthony Slide produced and directed a thirty-two minute documentary, *Portrait of Blanche Sweet.* He served as series consultant for the 20th Century-Fox/ABC series, *That's Hollywood;* as Hollywood advisor for the six-part Ulster Television series, *A Seat among the Stars: The*

Photograph by Andre de Toth

Cinema and Ireland; and as associate producer of the ABC Television special, *The Dark Side of Hollywood.* He is currently involved in the production of a documentary film on early women directors.

Born in Birmingham, England, in 1944, Anthony Slide's first professional involvement with film was as assistant editor of the British annual, *International Film Guide,* in 1968. He came to the United States in 1971 as a Louis B. Mayer Research Fellow with the American Film Institute's Center for Advanced Film Studies.

For relaxation, he reads mystery novels, cooks, and walks his dog, a labrador retriever, around the neighborhood in Studio City, California. The dog, whose name is Stuart, has the distinction of having been kissed by both Hurd Hatfield and Betty White. Anthony Slide has only been kissed by Betty White.